BEST OF

Dubrovnik

D1392484

Jeanne Oliver

How to use this book

Colour-Coding & Maps

Each chapter has a colour code along the banner at the top of the page which is also used for text and symbols on maps (eg all venues reviewed in the Highlights chapter are orange on the maps). The fold-out maps inside the front and back covers are numbered from 1 to 4. All sights and venues in the text have map references; eg (3, B3) means Map 3, grid reference B3. See p64 for map symbols.

Prices

Multiple prices listed with reviews (eg 10/5KN) usually indicate adult/concession admission to a venue. Concession prices can include senior, student, member or coupon discounts. Meal cost and room rate categories are listed at the start of the Eating and Sleeping chapters, respectively.

Text Symbols

- ☎ telephone
- ✉ address
- 🖥 email/website address
- € admission
- ⏱ opening hours
- ⓘ information
- Ⓜ metro
- 🚌 bus
- Ⓟ parking available
- ♿ wheelchair access
- ✖ on-site/nearby eatery
- ⛎ child-friendly venue
- Ⓥ good vegetarian selection

Best of Dubrovnik
1st edition – Jun 2006

Published by Lonely Planet Publications Pty Ltd
ABN 36 005 607 983

Australia Head Office, Locked Bag 1, Footscray, Vic 3011
☎ 03 8379 8000 fax 03 8379 8111
🖥 talk2us@lonelyplanet.com.au
USA 150 Linden St, Oakland, CA 94607
☎ 510 893 8555 toll free 800 275 8555
fax 510 893 8572
🖥 info@lonelyplanet.com
UK 72–82 Rosebery Avenue, London EC1R 4RW
☎ 020 7841 9000 fax 020 7841 9001
🖥 go@lonelyplanet.co.uk

This title was commissioned in Lonely Planet's London office by Fiona Buchan and produced by Cambridge Publishing Management Limited. **Thanks** to Glenn Beanland, David Burnett, Steven Cann, Piotr Czajkowski, Brendan Dempsey, Ryan Evans, Fayette Fox, Quentin Frayne, Michala Green, Mark Griffiths, Imogen Hall, Glenn van der Knijff, Anthony Phelan, Charles Rawlings-Way, Annika Roojun, Jessica Rose, Michael Ruff, Wibowo Rusli, Jacqui Saunders, Amanda Sierp, Fiona Siseman, Ray Thomson, Rachel Wood

Photographs by Lonely Planet Images and Richard Nebesky except for the following: p20 Jan Strommel/Lonely Planet Images, p25 Jon Davison/Lonely Planet Images, p26 Wayne Walton/Lonely Planet Images.

Cover photograph Sponza Palace at night, Johanna Huber/4Corners Images.

All images are copyright of the photographers unless otherwise indicated. Many of the images in this guide are available for licensing from Lonely Planet Images: www.lonelyplanetimages.com.

ISBN 1 74104 823 0

Printed through Colorcraft Ltd, Hong Kong.
Printed in China

Lonely Planet and the Lonely Planet logo are trademarks of Lonely Planet and are registered in the US Patent and Trademark Office and in other countries.

Lonely Planet does not allow its name or logo to be appropriated by commercial establishments, such as retailers, restaurants or hotels. Please let us know of any misuses: www.lonelyplanet.com/ip.

Contents

INTRODUCING DUBROVNIK 5
NEIGHBOURHOODS 6
ITINERARIES 7

HIGHLIGHTS 8
Placa 8
City Walls 10
Dominican Monastery & Museum 11
Franciscan Monastery & Museum 12
Rector's Palace 13
Cathedral of the Assumption of the
    Virgin 14
Sponza Palace 15

SIGHTS & ACTIVITIES 16
Museums 16
Churches & Synagogues 16
Buildings & Monuments 18
Public Spaces 20
Dubrovnik for Children 21

TRIPS & TOURS 22
Walking Tours 22
Day Trips 24
Organised Tours 26

SHOPPING 27
Shopping Centres 27
Markets 27
Arts & Crafts 27
Clothing & Jewellery 28
Music & Books 29
Food & Drink 29

EATING 30
Old Town 30
Lapad 34

ENTERTAINMENT 35
Bars & Pubs 35
Cafés 37
Dance Clubs & Discos 38
Cinemas 38
Rock, Jazz & Blues 38
Classical Music & Dance 39

SLEEPING 40
Deluxe 41
Top End 42
Midrange 42
Budget 44

ABOUT DUBROVNIK 45
History 45
Environment 47
Government & Politics 47
Economy 48
Society & Culture 48
Arts 48

DIRECTORY 51
INDEX 60
MAP LEGEND 64

From the Publisher

THE AUTHOR
Jeanne Oliver

Jeanne first visited Croatia for Lonely Planet in 1996, just as peace was settling over the country. Although bombs hadn't fallen on Dubrovnik for a number of years, tourists had yet to return and residents were anxious for their future. She returned in 1998 to write the first edition of Lonely Planet's *Croatia*, the first guidebook in English to the country, and noticed that much of Dubrovnik's beauty had already been restored. The city was re-energising as tourists slowly drifted back. Returning nearly every year since to update Lonely Planet guidebooks, she's watched Dubrovnik blossom into a major Mediterranean destination. From her home in the South of France, Jeanne writes frequently about Croatia.

LONELY PLANET AUTHORS

Why is our travel information the best in the world? It's simple: our authors are independent, dedicated travellers. They don't research using just the Internet or phone, and they don't take freebies in exchange for positive coverage. They travel widely, to all the popular spots and off the beaten track. They personally visit thousands of hotels, restaurants, cafés, bars, galleries, palaces, museums and more – and they take pride in getting all the details right, and telling it how it is. For more, see the authors section on **www.lonelyplanet.com**.

PHOTOGRAPHER
Richard Nebesky

Richard was born one snowy night in the grungy Prague suburb of Zizkov, but surprisingly he didn't have a camera in his hand. It was, however, not long after he got out of his cot that his father, an avid photo enthusiast, gave him his first point-and-shoot unit. Ever since, the camera has been by his side on wander treks, ski adventures and cycling trips, and while researching Lonely Planet books around the globe. He has also worked for various magazines and travel guide publishers and on many social photography projects.

Visiting Dubrovnik for the first time in 1985, it was love at first sight, with one of the most beautiful towns of the world. The place has it all! Beaches with crystal-clear blue water, great seafood and plenty of sights going back almost 1000 years. Due to its compactness, it is easy to photograph and its friendly and easygoing inhabitants make it a joy.

SEND US YOUR FEEDBACK

We love to hear from travellers – your comments keep us on our toes and help make our books better. Our well-travelled team reads every word on what you loved or loathed about this book. Although we cannot reply individually to postal submissions, we always guarantee that your feedback goes straight to the appropriate authors, in time for the next edition – and the most useful submissions are rewarded with a free book. To send us your updates – and find out about Lonely Planet events, newsletters and travel news – visit our award-winning website: **www.lonelyplanet.com/feedback**.

Note: We may edit, reproduce and incorporate your comments in Lonely Planet products such as guidebooks, websites and digital products, so let us know if you don't want your comments reproduced or your name acknowledged. For a copy of our privacy policy visit **www.lonelyplanet.com/privacy**.

Introducing Dubrovnik

Lord Byron proclaimed it 'the pearl of the Adriatic'. George Bernard Shaw said it was 'paradise on earth'. For a general under Napoleon it was an 'oasis of civilisation'. Each phrase describes one aspect of Dubrovnik's greatness but none captures them all. The marble streets and baroque buildings of Dubrovnik's Old Town emit a pearly light in the Adriatic sun. Beyond the city is a heavenly landscape of beaches, wooded peninsulas and a sea strewn with lush islands. And its curtain of walls protected a civilised, sophisticated republic that flourished in peace and prosperity for five centuries.

Although the shelling of Dubrovnik in 1991 horrified the world, the city has bounced back with characteristic vigour to enchant its visitors again. A walk around its walls offers heady views of Dubrovnik's unique land- and seascape. The hedonistic can pamper themselves in one of the city's fine hotels or enjoy a refreshing plunge into the sea. History buffs can trace the rise and fall of Dubrovnik's commercial empire in museums replete with art and artefacts. A local symphony orchestra and a busy concert season delight music-lovers. Whether it's the relaxed Mediterranean lifestyle, the interplay of light and stone, the fresh sea breezes or remarkable history, Dubrovnik is suffused with an ineffable magic that makes it one of the world's great destinations.

The white marble of Placa (p8) shimmers in the lamplight

Neighbourhoods

When people think of Dubrovnik, it's usually the **Old Town** they picture. The sober stone buildings lined up on either side of **Placa**, the floridly sculpted public buildings and, above all, the magnificent walls circling the city are point-and-shoot perfect. It's an architectural gem and drenched in history, but the Old Town is far from a museum. People live, bring up their kids and grow old in the baroque houses here. They shop in the local grocery stores and chat with their neighbours in local cafés. A flood of tourists and skyrocketing property values have made normal life difficult to sustain but people manage it nevertheless.

While all the museums and major sights are within the walls of the Old Town, nearly all the hotels are in the surrounding region. Along **Frana Supila**, just south of the Old Town, a handful of luxury hotels backed by steep hills line the coastline for about a kilometre. North of the Old Town, the main road, **Branitelja Dubrovnika**, climbs up a hill and then descends toward Gruž harbour, the docking point for boats and ferries. The **Gruž** neighbourhood that borders the harbour is a busy commercial district with a couple of restaurants and hotels.

> ### OFF THE BEATEN TRACK
> Dubrovnik's Old Town can be crowded in summer. If you need a breather you can head to lovely **Gradac Park** (p20). For the best views of the Old Town, take Frana Supila past the Hotel Argentina. Eventually you'll reach the St Jakov Monastery, now the Croatian Academy of Sciences. Behind the monastery 163 steps lead down to secluded **Sveti Jakov Beach** (p20).

Across the harbour lie **Lapad** and **Babin Kuk** peninsulas, where most of Dubrovnik's hotels are planted. The leafy interior of the Lapad is heavily residential but the large hotels have commandeered most of the coast. In summer, locals and visitors stroll on pedestrian **Kralja Zvonimira**, which has a busy café scene. Babin Kuk is undeveloped except for several sprawling resort-style hotels. There are also a few stores and restaurants here, and much shrubbery crisscrossed by gravel paths. Dubrovnik's largest beach, the Copacabana, is a major draw on the north shore of Babin Kuk.

Safe haven: boats moored in the shelter of the city walls (p10)

Itineraries

All of Dubrovnik's most celebrated sights are reachable on foot. Just walking through, around or above the Old Town reveals a wealth of architectural detail, while the reasonably priced museums offer a window into Dubrovnik's remarkable history.

DAY ONE

Enter through **Pile Gate** (p19) and walk down **Placa** (p8). Stop for a pastry at **Café Cele** (p37) and then tour the **City Walls** (p10). After your walk, have lunch at **Dundo Maroje** (p31) and then visit the **Dominican Monastery** (p11) before taking a walk on Frana Supila to admire the views of the Old Town. Have a romantic cocktail at the rooftop terrace at **Revelin Fort** (p19) before following one of our dinner recommendations (pp30–34).

DAY TWO

Start at the **Rector's Palace** (p13) for an overview of Dubrovnik's history. Afterwards, take time out for some people-watching over coffee at **Gradska Kavana** (p37) before moving on to admire Dubrovnik's **Cathedral** (p14). Visit **Sponza Palace** (p15) and the **Franciscan Monastery** (p12) before

Massive Minčeta Tower (p10) has stood guard over Dubrovnik for 600 years

taking a lunch break in town. After lunch visit **War Photos Limited** (p16) and then head to the art treasures of Dubrovnik's **churches** (p16). Watch the sunset from romantic **Cafe Buza** (p35).

DAY THREE

Enjoy the beauty of the Dubrovnik region. Take a boat trip to **Mljet Island National Park** (p24) and bike around the lakes, or take a day trip to **Lokrum** (p24) to sprawl on the rocky shore. It's even easier to choose one of the **beaches** around town (p20) to rest up for Dubrovnik's **nightlife** (pp35–39).

WORST OF DUBROVNIK

- Elbow-to-elbow crowds on Placa in high season
- Lack of interesting and unique souvenirs
- Summer traffic jams on roads leading to the Old Town

PLACA (3, B2–D3)

Your first view of Placa (pronounced platsa) is not unlike seeing Venice for the first time. There's simply no other place like it in the world. The hard, white stone catches the sunlight and seems to bathe the whole town in a warm, white aura. When it rains, the moisture adds a sheen to the stone and by moonlight the street shimmers under the glow of street lamps. Placa is also called Stradun, allegedly because an officer in the Austro-Hungarian army saw it and exclaimed '*Che stradone*', which translates as 'What a big street!'

Placa: stroll, shop or just marvel at its beauty

For centuries, Placa has been Dubrovnik's main street for processions and festivals, as well as for shopping and strolling. It was created in the 11th century when a channel that separated an islet from the mainland was filled in. It was initially paved with brick, and stones were added in the 15th century. It was re-paved in 1901 but the shelling of Dubrovnik in 1991 blasted holes in much of it. When the smoke had cleared, white stone hastily quarried from nearby islands was used to patch up the street.

The buildings lining the street once looked very much like **Sponza Palace** (p15) but nearly all the Renaissance features of Dubrovnik were destroyed in the devastating earthquake of 1667. Hasty reconstruction gave the street its striking architectural unity. All buildings lining the street are in baroque style, with identical façades of uniform height, and each was designed to incorporate a shop or café at ground level: city planners wanted to make sure that Placa remained a busy, commercial street.

Placa also contains some of Dubrovnik's most recognisable landmarks. At the northern end is the **Onofrio Fountain**, built in 1438 as part of a water-supply system that involved bringing water from a well 12km away. The system still works and provided the city's residents with drinking water in 1991, when Serb attackers put the larger water system out of action. Of the sculpture that originally adorned the fountain, only 16 carved masks spouting water survived the 1667 earthquake. The fountain was sited near Pile Gate, the main entrance to the city, in order to encourage visitors to wash themselves before walking around.

The southern end of Placa is marked by the Gothic-Renaissance **Clock Tower**. Built in 1446, it was restored many times and rebuilt in 1929. Since the 15th century, two little green men in the tower have rung out the hours. Called Maro and Baro, the original bronze figures are now in Sponza Palace. The digital clock in the shaft was inserted in 1929.

At the foot of the Clock Tower is **Luža Square**. In the middle of the square is the **Orlando Column**, where edicts were read and verdicts announced under the Ragusan Republic (p46). Orlando is the Italianised name of Roland, hero of the medieval French epic poem, *Chanson de Roland.* What

Meet up at the Orlando column

is a French hero doing in Dubrovnik? According to legend, Roland defended Dubrovnik against Saracen invaders in the 9th century. If it were true it would have been quite a feat, since Roland died in 778. But the legend lives on and Roland grew to become a symbol of the free state. Carved in 1417, the forearm of the medieval knight was the official linear measure of the Republic. Now, the column is a popular meeting place.

Nearby is **Little Onofrio's Fountain**, part of the same water-supply system as its larger cousin to the west but built to supply water to the marketplace on Luža Square. It is currently serving the hygienic needs of Dubrovnik's extensive pigeon population.

DON'T MISS

- Strolling along Placa at night, when the white marble streets gleam in the lamplight
- The opening of Dubrovnik's prestigious Summer Festival (p39) on Luža Square
- Sipping a drink at one of Placa's outdoor cafés

CITY WALLS (3, B2)

The 2km-long city walls that completely enclose Dubrovnik are the city's most striking feature. Built between the 13th and 16th centuries and still intact today, these powerful walls are the finest in the Mediterranean and Dubrovnik's main claim to fame.

The ancient core of the city was already protected by a fortification system in the 9th century. As Dubrovnik expanded, the walls were extended and, by the 13th century, most of the city was enclosed by walls 1.5m thick. At the end of the 14th century, Dubrovnik broke free from Venice's protection. This prompted it to reinforce its defences. Fifteen square forts were added to the walls and work was begun on the circular **Minčeta Tower.** The menacing rise of the Ottoman Empire in the 15th century led the city to pile even more stone onto its defences, strengthening the existing forts and adding new ones. Fearing attack by land, the builders ensured that the walls were stronger on the land side, where they are up to 6m thick, in contrast to the sea side, where they are 1.5m to 3m thick.

The walls endured nearly unchanged for five centuries but came under serious rocket attack in 1991. The city's attackers managed to score 111 direct hits on the walls. All has now been repaired and visitors can once again enjoy unrivalled views of the Old Town and the Adriatic from its ramparts.

INFORMATION
€ 30/10KN ⏲ 9am-6.30pm Apr-Oct & 9am-4pm Nov-Mar

BOKAR TOWER (3, A3)

When Bokar Tower was built in the 15th century, it represented the latest and most modern ideas in fortress design. Until then, forts were square but Dubrovnik needed a better system to protect its western side. The pioneering circular design allowed more cannons to be positioned and thus offered protection to a larger area. The tower was so solidly constructed that its walls appear to rise from the sea floor and expand into the rocky cliff that supports it. Yet, the ports were placed low enough for the cannons to fire straight out at potential attackers.

DOMINICAN MONASTERY & MUSEUM (3, E2–3)

This architectural highlight, in a transitional Gothic-Renaissance style, has a rich trove of paintings. Built in the 14th century, at the same time as the city walls, the stark exterior resembles a fortress more than a religious complex. The citizens of Dubrovnik built the monastery but the monks mortared in the columns of the stairway balustrade in order to prevent Dubrovnik's men from looking at the ankles of women as they entered the church.

The interior contains an exquisite 15th-century **cloister** constructed by local artisans after the designs of the Florentine architect Massa di Bartolomeo. Within the embellished Gothic arcades, orange and palm trees provide shade for contemplation. From the cloister, you enter a large, single-naved **church** with an immense Byzantine-style crucifix that was given to the church in 1394 after an epidemic of plague. In addition to harbouring elaborate silver reliquaries, the church was also a prestigious burial place for the Ragusan nobility whose tombs are placed throughout the church. The eastern wing of the monastery contains an impressive art **museum**, which contains paintings by Dubrovnik's finest 15th- and 16th-century artists, including Božidarević, Dobričević and Hamzić. The brothers of this monastery were particularly interested in collecting art, especially by local artists. Notice the tryptich by Nikola Božidarević, which shows St Blaise holding pre-earthquake Dubrovnik in his hand, and his *Madonna and Child* altarpiece.

INFORMATION
- ☎ 426 472
- ✉ off Svetog Dominika 4
- € 15/7KN
- ◷ 9am-6pm

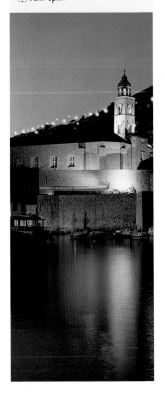

DON'T MISS
- The elaborate cistern crown in the monastery courtyard
- The pastel of St Dominic by Cavtat artist Vlaho Bukovac in the church
- Titian's painting of Mary Magdalene in the sacristy

FRANCISCAN MONASTERY & MUSEUM (3, B2)

This vast monastery, which stretches from Placa to the Minčeta Tower, is one of Dubrovnik's most cherished sights. It was begun in the 14th century, Dubrovnik's 'Golden Age', but most of it was destroyed in the 1667 earthquake. Much of what you see dates from the 17th-century reconstruction. The façade is relatively sober except for the remarkable *Pietà* over the entrance. Sculpted in 1498 by the local masters Petar and Leonard Andrijić, the *Pietà* is flanked by St Jerome and St John the Baptist and topped by a benevolent Creator. The monastery is currently run by seven friars.

Inside the monastery complex is the mid-14th-century **cloister**, one of the most important late-Romanesque structures in Dalmatia. The rows of double arches create a hypnotically beautiful effect. Notice how each capital over the double columns is topped by a different figure, portraying human heads, animals and floral arrangements. In the centre of the cloister, the friars planted herbs and fruit trees to keep the monastery supplied with fresh produce.

DON'T MISS
- The richly decorated sarcophagus of a Ragusan nobleman in the eastern gallery of the Cloister
- The painting of Dubrovnik before the earthquake in the monastery museum
- The collection of creams made according to local recipes in the pharmacy

Further inside you'll find the third-oldest functioning **pharmacy** in Europe. In business since 1391, it may have been the first pharmacy in Europe to open to the general public. On the counter is a rare aspirin box created to advertise the novelty of aspirin in pill form rather than powder. Before leaving, visit the **monastery museum**, with its collection of relics, liturgical objects, paintings, gold work and pharmacy items such as laboratory gear and medical books.

INFORMATION
☎ 426 345 ✉ Placa 2 € 10/5KN ⏰ 9am-6pm

RECTOR'S PALACE (3, D4)

This elegant 15th-century building was erected on the site of an old fort in order to house the rector, Dubrovnik's ruler. Though predominantly Gothic, it also contains Renaissance elements, particularly in the lavishly sculptured capitals on the exterior porch. Despite the mixture of styles, it retains a striking compositional unity.

The interior atrium features a splendid baroque staircase and a statue of Miho Pracat, who bequeathed one tonne of gold to the Republic and was the only commoner in the 1000 years of its existence to be honoured with a statue (1638).

The rest of the palace contains the rector's office and private chambers, as well as public halls and administrative offices.

INFORMATION
☎ 426 469
✉ Pred Dvorom 3
€ 20/7KN
🕒 9am-6pm

Interestingly, the elected rector was not permitted to leave the building during his one-month term without the permission of the senate. The palace is now a **museum**, with artfully restored rooms, portraits, coats of arms and coins, all of which evoke the glorious history of Dubrovnik.

Perfect proportions: the Gothic-Renaissance Rector's Palace

DON'T MISS
- The exquisite 17th-century cabinet decorated with gilt and painted glass in the museum
- The long lock of hair over the left shoulder of the rector mannequin, which indicated that a Ragusan senator was now serving his one-month term as rector
- The inscription over the main council chamber that reminds legislators to 'Forget private affairs. Think only of the general welfare.'

CATHEDRAL OF THE ASSUMPTION OF THE VIRGIN (3, D4)

The cathedral is an exuberant baroque confection

The origins of the cathedral are steeped in legend. Certainly there was a church here from the 7th century. Locals insist that in the 12th century Richard the Lionheart paid for its enlargement in gratitude to the people who saved him from a shipwreck near Lokrum. Whatever the truth, that church was destroyed in the 17th-century earthquake and work on the new church began immediately. A succession of Roman builders applied baroque style to the exterior, slathering it with columns, corniches and a statue-topped balustrade. The

INFORMATION
☎ 411 715
✉ Poljana M Drižća
€ Treasury 7/4KN
☼ 8am-8pm Mon-Sat, 11am-8pm Sun

interior is equally impressive, especially the altars. Notice the altar of St John Nepomuk, made of violet marble. The tiny **treasury** was secured by three keys kept by the archbishop, the cathedral rector and the Secretary of the Republic. Only if the keys were used simultaneously could the treasury be entered. Inside are no fewer than 138 gold and silver reliquaries: among the holy relics that they hold are the head, arms and a leg of St Blaise plus a fragment of the Holy Cross.

DON'T MISS
- Over the main altar, the polyptych of the *Assumption of the Virgin* made in Titian's studio. The white-haired figure in the centre is believed to be a portrait of Titian
- The 16th-century *Adoration of the Magi* triptych in the Treasury, which was used as a portable altar by Dubrovnik diplomats
- The *Madonna della Seggiola*, a copy of Raphael's original painting, now in the Pitti Palace in Florence. Some say that the copy was made by Raphael himself

SPONZA PALACE (3, D3)

Finally a building that wasn't destroyed in the 1667 earthquake! Fronted by an exquisite Renaissance portico resting on six columns, this superb structure is in a mixture of Gothic and Renaissance styles. The first floor has late-Gothic windows and the second-floor windows are in a Renaissance style, with an alcove containing a statue of St Blaise.

Sponza Palace was built in 1516 as a customs house and its interior court soon became a meeting hall for local merchants and businessmen. An inscription on the main arch reminds them of their obligations: 'When I measure the goods, the Lord measures with me'. Later, the building also housed the mint, the state treasury and a bank. Now it houses the state archives, a priceless repository of Dubrovnik's history. The collection includes 7000 volumes of manuscripts, 100,000 individual manuscripts and volumes of law books. Many date back nearly 1000 years. The legal documents in a dozen languages, shipping records, passenger and cargo lists testify to the scope of Dubrovnik's trading business. There's also a poignant Memorial Room of the Dubrovnik Defenders, commemorating those who lost their lives defending the city in the early 1990s.

INFORMATION
- ☎ 321 032
- ✉ Luža Square
- € free
- ☻ 9am-1pm & 6-8pm Mon-Fri, 8am-1pm Sat

THE EARTHQUAKE OF 1667

By the early 17th century, Dubrovnik was already rivalled by other maritime powers and its importance was being eroded by the opening of new trade routes to the East, but the final blow was the devastating earthquake on 6 August 1667. More than 5000 inhabitants perished as its Renaissance centre collapsed into rubble and fire swept the city. Even its great fleet anchored offshore was destroyed. Although the city rebuilt – in a splendid Roman baroque style – and pieced together its economy, it was never to recover its former glory. A much milder quake that damaged 45 houses in September 1995 reminded Dubrovnik's inhabitants of the vulnerability of their city.

Sights & Activities

MUSEUMS

Maritime Museum (3, F4)
The setting of the museum is St John Fort, which is probably more interesting than the exhibits evoking Dubrovnik's maritime history. Old salts may enjoy the ship models, musty old maps, paintings and strange navigational objects. Whatever floats your boat.
☎ 426 465
✉ St John Fort € 20/7KN
☉ 9am-6pm

Museum of Modern Art (2, F5)
Many of Dubrovnik's older art treasures are gracing the walls of the Dominican Monastery and the cathedral but this museum is a good place to get an overview of the city's modern artists, most notably Vlaho Bukovac, Marko Rešica, Ivo Dulčić and Antun Masle. Watch the schedule for temporary exhibitions (on the ground floor).
☎ 426 590

✉ Frana Supila 23 € free
☉ 10am-1pm & 5-9pm Tue-Sun

Rupe Ethnographic Museum (3, B4)
In 16th-century Dubrovnik, grain storage was a serious matter. This former granary contains 15 cisterns, each of which stored 1200 tonnes of grain. In addition to its historical interest, the building contains a small ethnographic museum displaying period costumes, photos and agricultural implements.
☎ 412 545 ✉ Od Rupa € 15/7KN ☉ 9am-6pm

War Photos Limited (3, C3)
Managed by former photojournalist Wade Goddard, the award-winning photos on display here concentrate on the subtleties of human violence rather than on its carnage. The permanent exhibition focuses on the Balkan wars but temporary exhibits include other conflicts. It's strong

medicine and may not be suitable for children but you won't easily forget this museum.
☎ 326 166 ✉ Antuninska 6 € 25KN ☉ 9am-9pm May-Oct, 10am-4pm Tue-Sat & 10am-2pm Sun Mar, Apr & Oct

CHURCHES & SYNAGOGUES

St Saviour Church (3, B2)
This small church next to the Franciscan Monastery was built in 1520 and survived the 1667 earthquake relatively intact. The exterior is in a pure Renaissance style and the single nave has Gothic vaulting. It makes a lovely setting for occasional performances by the Dubrovnik String Quartet.
✉ Placa ☉ Sunday mass and concerts

St Nicholas Church (3, D3)
The patron saint of sailors is honoured by this little gem. Begun in the 11th century,

Corn dollies at the Rupe Ethnographic Museum

it was rebuilt several times and now has a Renaissance façade. The interior contains Madonna paintings from the 13th and 14th centuries and a 16th-century wood relief of St Andrew.

✉ Zlatarska 2
☺ occasional evenings

St Blaise's Church (3, D3)
The church of Dubrovnik's patron saint perfectly reflects the city's soul: tastefully ornamented yet modest, stately yet welcoming. St Blaise's is Dubrovnik's most beloved church and the centre of the city's spiritual life. Built in a baroque style, it replaced an earlier church destroyed in the 1667 earthquake. Its ornate exterior contrasts strongly with the sober residences surrounding it. The interior is notable for its marble altars and a 15th-century silver gilt statue of St Blaise, who holds a model of pre-earthquake Dubrovnik. The artist Ivo Dulčić designed the stained-glass windows, which depict saints Peter, Paul, Cyril and Methodius.

✉ Luža Square ☺ morning & late-afternoon Mass Mon-Sat

St Ignatius Church
(3, C5)
The best part of this 18th-century church is the grandiose balustraded staircase leading up to it. The Roman architect who built it in 1738 was clearly inspired by the Spanish Steps in his home town. The Jesuit community financed the church's construction, decorating the interior with frescoes depicting scenes

DUBROVNIK'S PATRON SAINT
Statues and paintings of St Blaise, the bishop of Armenia who was martyred under Emperor Diocletian, are scattered throughout Dubrovnik, adorning all city gates and fortresses. In the 10th century he became Dubrovnik's patron saint after he allegedly appeared to the Cathedral's rector in a dream, warning that the Venetians were about to attack the city. His feast day is February 3 and all Dubrovnik turns out to celebrate. Processions of local dignitaries carry his relics through the streets, St Blaise's Church is spectacularly illuminated and the saint's flag flies from the top of the Orlando Column in Luža Square.

from the life of St Ignatius, founder of the Jesuit order.
✉ Uz Jezuite Poljana R. Boškovića ☺ early-evening Mass

Serbian Orthodox Church & Museum
(3, C3)
The church dates from 1877 and the museum next door contains a fascinating collection of icons from Crete,

Italy, Russia and Slovenia dating from the 15th to the 19th centuries. There are also several portraits by Vlaho Bukovac.
☎ 426 260 ✉ Od Puča 8
€ 10/5KN ☺ 9am-2pm Mon-Sat

Synagogue (3, D2)
Created in the 15th century, it's the oldest Sephardic and the second-oldest

JEWS IN DUBROVNIK

Although Jews in Dubrovnik number only about 50 today, their presence in the city extends back to the 14th century. After the Spanish Inquisition in the 16th century their numbers increased, even though Jews were confined to a locked ghetto and considered second-class citizens. When Napoleon seized Dubrovnik in 1806 he ended racially discriminatory laws but freedoms were revoked when France was defeated in 1814. Dubrovnik's Jewish community struggled throughout the 19th century and faced new hardships when the city was seized by Italy in 1941. After heavy pressure from the Germans, the Italians finally deported Dubrovnik's Jews in 1943. Many then joined Tito's Partizans in fighting the Axis powers.

synagogue in Europe. It's located on Žudioska (Jew Street) which was once gated at either end. There's a museum that displays sacred objects such as a 14th-century Torah. When the Nazis occupied Dubrovnik in 1943, the synagogue's holy objects were secreted in special chambers behind the walls.
☎ 412 219 ✉ Žudioska 5
🕙 10am-8pm Mon-Fri

BUILDINGS & MONUMENTS

Convent of St Clare (3, B3)
Don't just hurry to Restaurant Jadran (p33), stop and look at the surrounding architectural ensemble. This used to be the Convent of St Clare, built in the 13th century and then turned into Dubrovnik's first orphanage in the 15th century. Incredibly, Napoleon used it as a stable in the 19th century.
✉ Poljana P. Miličevića

St John Fort (3, F4)
With treasure-laden ships coming and going, Dubrovnik's Old Harbour needed protection. The St John Fort was begun in the 14th century and modified a few times until it finally took shape in the 16th century. The sea side is rounded and the land side is flat but both have enough gun ports to discourage any potential troublemaker. Within the fortress is the Maritime Museum (p16) and the Aquarium (p21).

Lazareti (2, F5)
The bars on the windows are the clue that you're not just looking at another monastery. Built between 1590 and 1624, this well-preserved cluster of houses served as a quarantine quarter for visitors from the East, especially Turkey. Visitors from the West were held in quarantine in Danče

but the buildings no longer exist. Lazareti now houses a few artisan studios and small stages for alternative arts events.

✉ Frana Supila

Lovrijenac Fort (2, E5)

Lonely Lovrijenac Fort looms over the Old Town like Banquo's ghost, reminding everyone that Dubrovnik's riches once required constant vigilance. Built and rebuilt from the 14th to the 17th century, the venerable fort becomes Elsinore each summer when the Dubrovnik Summer Festival (p39) stages its annual production

St Blaise looks down from Pile Gate

of *Hamlet*. In fact, Croatian heart-throb Goran Višnjić got his start playing the title role here. Notice the Latin inscription over the entrance, which translates as 'Freedom is not sold for all the gold in the world.'

✉ Lovrijenac
€ included with ticket to City Walls, otherwise 10KN
☼ as City Walls (p10)

Pile Gate (3, B2)

A benevolent St Blaise (p17) in a niche over the entrance blesses all who pass beneath but first Dubrovnik's visitors had to cross a protective moat that ran around the city walls. The 14th-century stone bridge leads to a wooden drawbridge and a solid gate. If there was an urgent need for someone to enter or leave after hours, a small portion of the right gate opened just enough for someone to pass through. Beyond the outer gate is an inner gate with a statue of St Blaise carved by Croatia's most famous sculptor, Ivan Meštrović.

Ploče Gate (3, E2)

Like Pile Gate on the west side of the Old Town, Ploče

Dubrovnik's strongest fortress, Revelin Fort (p20)

Had enough sightseeing? Head for one of Dubrovnik's fabulous beaches

Gate, its counterpart on the east side, also has inner and outer gates that lead to a stone bridge spanning the moat. Revelin Fort added further protection to the city's eastern aspect.

Revelin Fort (3, F2)

In 1538, the Dubrovnik senate saw the rise of the Ottoman Empire as an urgent threat and immediately ordered the reinforcement of the 15th-century Revelin Fort that protected Ploče Gate. Thrown up in only 11 years, it became Dubrovnik's strongest fortress, so well built that it survived the 1667 earthquake intact and so secure that it housed Dubrovnik's treasury. Notice how the only land access is by bridges that cross a moat. The Dubrovnik Summer Festival now stages concerts and plays on the spacious rooftop terrace.

PUBLIC SPACES

Banje Beach (2, F5)

The gravel here is the closest Dubrovnik gets to sand and the beach's location near Lazareti (p18) makes it a convenient R & R stop after sightseeing in the Old Town. If you want to stretch out on a lounge chair, you'll have to rent it from the EastWest Club (p36) but you will get a matchless view of Dubrovnik's eastern walls.

Copacabana Beach (2, A2)

On the Babin Kuk Peninsula, this is Dubrovnik's largest beach and ground zero for watersports. You can dive, waterski, paddle around, windsurf or just enjoy the clean, blue water. There's also a slithery toboggan for kids.

Lapad Beaches (2, A3–B3)

Sumratin Bay is bordered by pebble beaches that stretch from the small cove in front of the Hotel Splendid (p43) to the larger beach in front of the Grand Hotel Park. They tend to be crowded with hotel guests in the summer but you can usually find a space.

Gundulićeva Poljana (3, D4)

Surrounded by stately Baroque houses, this attractive square hosts a daily morning market and open-air concerts during the Dubrovnik Summer Festival. The monument in the centre commemorates Dubrovnik's famous poet,

Ivan Gundulić, and the reliefs on the pedestal depict scenes from his epic poem, *Osman*.

Gradac Park (2, E5)
Even before mass tourism arrived, residents of Dubrovnik sometimes needed to escape their walled city. Built in the 19th century when Dubrovnik was part of the Austrian Empire, this graceful park west of town is bisected by a tree-lined promenade from which you can enjoy the view over the Adriatic. All is quiet except for birdsong and a gently splashing fountain.

Sveti Jakov Beach (2, off F5)
Take Frana Supila east past the big hotels until you come to the former St Jakov Monastery. Go a few more metres and you'll see steep steps (163 of them) leading down to Sveti Jakov Beach, a summer favourite with the locals.

DUBROVNIK FOR CHILDREN

You'll often see local kids kicking a football around in one of Old Town's squares but there's little here of particular interest to tiny travellers. However, just outside Old Town is **Banje Beach** (see opposite) where kids can splash in the sea. On the opposite side of town is **Gradac Park** with woodsy areas to explore. The best area for families is Babin Kuk peninsula. **Copacabana beach** (see

The baroque altar of St Blaise's Church (p17): your cherubs may prefer the beach

opposite) has relatively shallow offshore waters, a toboggan and a variety of watersports activities. Hotels Argosy (p42) and Minčeta (p43) are specially geared to families, offering children's activities, playgrounds and children's pools. All the hotels in Babin Kuk are used to dealing with families and can easily arrange babysitting services, which is not necessarily the case in other Dubrovnik hotels. If you stay in a private apartment

however, you can usually arrange with the owner to look after the kids while you explore the town.

Aquarium (3, F4)
Adults might not be too impressed but kids usually like to watch the old sea turtle paddle around. There are also a few other tanks that conjure up underwater life in the Adriatic.
☎ 427 937 ⊠ St John Fort at Kneza Damjana Jude 2 € 20/10KN ☼ 9am-8pm

Built into the walls of St John Fort, the aquarium's tanks are fed with fresh sea water

Trips & Tours

WALKING TOURS
Old Town Sights

Begin your walk by passing through **Pile Gate** (**1**; p19) and take a walk around the **City Walls** (**2**; p10). Leave the walls where you entered and walk on to **Placa**, Dubrovnik's wonderful main pedestrian avenue. First you'll notice the **Onofrio Fountain** (**3**; p8) while on your left is elegant **St Saviour Church** (**4**; p16). Next to it is the **Franciscan Monastery and Museum** (**5**; p12) with its marvellous cloister. Proceed down Placa. Near the end is the **Orlando Column** (**6**; p9) and ahead of you is the **Clock Tower** (**7**; p9), at the end of Placa. To your left is **Sponza Palace** (**8**; p15) and to your right **Little Onofrio's Fountain** (**9**; p9). On the other side of Luža Square is **St Blaise's Church** (**10**; p17). Leave the square, turning right onto Pred Dvorom and visit the **Rector's Palace** (**11**; p13). Next, turn left and then right to admire **Gundulićeva Poljana** (**12**; p20). Backtrack to Pred Dvorom, turn right and head to the **Cathedral of**

The dome of St Blaise's Church (p17)

the Assumption of the Virgin (**13**; p14), which rises before you in all its baroque splendour. When you leave the church, return to Placa and pass under the **Customs Gate** (**14**). Follow Svetog Domenika for about 25m and you'll come to the entrance to the **Dominican Monastery** (**15**; p11) on your left. Feast your eyes on Dubrovnik's finest art collection and leave the Old Town by **Ploče Gate** (**16**; p19).

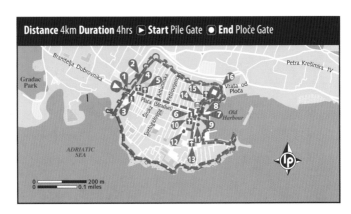

Distance 4km **Duration** 4hrs ▶ **Start** Pile Gate ● **End** Ploče Gate

Hidden Dubrovnik

Start at the **Onofrio Fountain** (**1**; p8) and head down Placa. Pass Garište on your right, noticing the **archways** (**2**) that link the upper floors of the buildings. Turn right on Zlatarićeva. The low windows on the left are a vestige of the **state orphanage** (**3**) that took in unwanted children from 1434. Although now mortared over, there was a wheel here upon which veiled women would place their babies at night. The wall inscription is from Psalm 39. Cross Od Puča and on the right is a **Latin inscription** (**4**) from 1597 that translates as 'Peace be with you who play ball. Remember that you will die for your sins.' Continue to Za Rokum and you will see that the ballplaying continues. On the right is the Renaissance **St Roch (Rokum) Church** (**5**). Turn left on Za Rokum. At the end of the street is the **All Saints (Domino) Church** (**6**), seat of the fraternity of the stonemasons. Notice the tablet on the outer wall inscribed to the 'Confraternità dei Muratori' (Stonemasons' Guild), with the mortar trowel as part of their emblem. Adjacent is the **birthplace of Marin Držić** (**7**), Dubrovnik's most renowned playwright. Continue up Od Domina and turn right at Od Rupa to visit the **Rupe Ethnographic Museum** (**8**; p16). Then, turn left and mount Od Šorte to Od Kaštela and the former **St Mary's Convent** (**9**), now turned into social housing. Notice the coat of arms of Dubrovnik over the entrance. Continue along Od Kaštela and turn left down Svete Marije. Make a right and a quick left to go down Svetog Josipa. At the corner of Od Puča is the Renaissance **Martinusic Palace** (**10**) with the family's coat of arms emblazoned on the second-floor corner.

Distance 1km **Duration** 1hr
▶ **Start** Onofrio Fountain
● **End** Od Puča and Svetog Josipa

A city landmark: the Onofrio Fountain (p8)

DAY TRIPS
Mljet National Park (4)

Ancient Greeks called the island Melita, meaning 'honey', and it really is a honey of an island. Nearly three-quarters of the island is covered by forests and the rest is dotted with fields, vineyards and small villages. The western half of the island is a tranquil national park where the lush vegetation is unmarred by the trappings of tourism. There are two lovely saltwater lakes, Malo Jezero and Veliko Jezero. In the middle of Veliko Jezero is a much photographed monastery that is now a restaurant.

INFORMATION
40km east of Dubrovnik

- 🚢 There's a regular ferry Monday to Saturday (32KN, 2 hours) that docks at Sobra. Buses take you to the entrances to the national park at Polače and Pomena. There's also a small passenger boat, the *Nona Ana* (2, C3), that leaves for Polače in the morning and returns in the afternoon (50KN, 1³/₄ hours)
- ℹ️ in Polače (☎ 744 125; 🖥 www. np-mljet.hr; ⏲ 8am-1pm Mon-Fri Oct-May, 8am-8pm Mon-Sat & 8am-1pm Sun Jun-Sep)
- € 90/30KN including the boat trip to the monastery

Lokrum Island (1, C2)

Deeply green and forested, Lokrum is Dubrovnik's most popular offshore destination. Nudies come for the naturist beach at the tip of the island while the clad crowd fills the rocky coves around the island or baths in Mrtvo More, a salty inland pond. Inland, there's a Benedictine monastery and a botanic garden in the midst of palms and cacti. There are no hotels, roads or cars on the island but there is a restaurant and café in the ruins of the monastery (summer only).

INFORMATION
680m southwest of Dubrovnik

- 🚢 Regular excursion boats leave from Dubrovnik's Old Harbour (3, E3; 80KN return, 30 minutes). They run hourly in summer and a few times a day off-season.

Lopud (1, C2)

Part of the Elafiti archipelago, Lopud is known for having the best beach in the region. Šunj Beach is on a sheltered cove with fine white sand that stretches gently out to the sea, making it perfect for small kids and waders. There's a small settlement along the harbour with a few restaurants and a hotel but the rest of the island is sparsely inhabited. The lush vegetation, composed of cypresses, citrus trees and palms, makes the island exceptionally attractive for strolling and hiking.

INFORMATION
11km northwest of Dubrovnik

- Daily car ferries connect Dubrovnik with Lopud (2, C3; 13KN, 50 minutes, 6 daily). The passenger boat *Nona Ana* runs on Saturday (13KN, 35 minutes)
- Tourist office (☎ 759 086; ☺ 8am-1pm & 5-7pm Mon-Fri, 9am-noon Sat, Sun)

Cavtat (1, C2)

Cavtat is a small town that curves around an attractive harbour bordered by pebble beaches. The atmosphere is peaceful and the luxuriant vegetation freshens the air. It's known as the birthplace of Vlaho Bukovac (1855–1922), Croatia's most renowned modern painter. His home has been turned into a small museum. Another famous sight is the mausoleum of the Račić family, designed and built by Ivan Meštrović.

INFORMATION
21km southeast of Dubrovnik

- bus 10 runs hourly to Cavtat (15KN, 45 minutes)
- in summer, there are boats from the Old Harbour (3, C3; 80KN return, 1 hour)
- Tourist Office (☎ 479 025; 🖳 www.tzcavtat-konavle.hr; ✉ Tiha 3; ☺ 8am-3pm Mon-Fri & 9am-noon Sat Sep-Jun, 8am-6pm daily Jul & Aug)

ORGANISED TOURS

Adria Adventure (2, B3)
Whether you're just dipping into the sport or are an experienced kayaker, this company has a kayak tour for you. Newbies may want to start with an easy one-day paddle to Lokrum Island (p24) or a weekend exploring the Elafiti Islands. More experienced kayakers should consider a week of paddling around the Elafiti Islands (right).
☎ 098-438 888 ☐ www.adriatic-sea-kayak.com
✉ Masarykov put 9 (beach)
€ €35-410

Atlas Travel Agency (3, A2)
With an array of guides, boats and buses at its disposal, Atlas Travel Agency is well equipped to show you all Dubrovnik's regional highlights. You can take a guided walking tour of the Old Town, a bus trip to Mostar or Međugorje in Bosnia & Hercegovina, or to the Montenegro coast, a wine tour of the Pelješac Peninsula, a boat ride along the Neretva River or longer boat trips to Mljet and Korčula.
☎ 442 574 ☐ www.atlas-croatia.com ✉ Sv Đurđa 1
€ €40-120 ⏱ 10am-6pm

Elafiti Islands (1, B2)
Lopud (p25) is only one of the 13 gorgeous Elafiti Islands, each with its own special flavour. On a boat tour, you'll have a chance to swim at Šunj Beach on Lopud and to visit tiny Koločep, noted for its forests, vineyards and orchards. Šipan, the largest island, is favourite with the Dubrovnik aristocracy, who built houses there in the 15th century. The boat lands in Šipanska Luka, where there are remains of a Roman villa and a 15th-century Gothic duke's palace.
🚤 boats leave from Dubrovnik's Old Harbour for an all-day excursion (3, E3; 250KN)

Navis Underwater Explorers (2, A2)
From their base on Copacabana Beach, this scuba-diving operation organises offshore exploration. The most famous underwater sight is the wreck of the *Tavanta*, sunk in 1943, but there's also great diving around St Andrija, in the Elafiti Islands.
☎ 099-350 2773
☐ navis@dv.t-c.m.hr
✉ Copacabana Beach
€ from €40

Take a hike – or a dip – on the island of Lopud (p25)

Shopping

Dubrovnik's cultivated residents tended to lean more towards the fine arts, architecture and sculpture than artisanship, and this has left the city without a tradition of locally produced handicrafts. Now that Dubrovnik has begun to attract well-heeled foreign and domestic tourists, some of Croatia's cutting-edge designers are opening jewellery and clothes shops in the Old Town. Traditional Croatian embroidered fabrics are displayed in a number of shops, including the rather ho-hum souvenir shops along Placa.

SHOPPING CENTRES

Konzum (2, C3)
Just behind the bus station is this modern supermarket, the largest one in Dubrovnik. Local wines are cheaper here than in the speciality shops but there is less variety. On the plus side, you can buy your bottles and hop directly onto your bus or boat.
⊠ Obabla Pape Ivana Pavla III ⏰ 8am-7pm Mon-Sat, 8am-1pm Sun

Lapad Shopping Centre (2, B3)
There's nothing particularly Croatian about this new, modern multi-level shopping centre but, if you're out in Lapad and need to replace your sandals or buy a raincoat, it's an indispensable stop.
⊠ Kralja Tomislava ⏰ 9am-7.30pm Mon-Fri, 10am-2pm Sat

MARKETS

Gruž Market (2, D3)
This morning market is crammed with locals stocking their shopping baskets with the freshest regional produce or inspecting last night's catch at the fish stand. Prices are more reasonable than the market at Gundulić Square and there's a wider selection.
⊠ Pape Ivana Pavla II ⏰ 7am-1pm Mon-Sat

Morning Market (3, D4)
The fruit and vegetable stands clustered around the statue of Ivan Gundulić, Dubrovnik's famous poet (p49), in the centre of this large square are popular with camera-clickers. It's becoming a little touristy; prices are better at Gruž Market.
⊠ Gundulićeva Poljana ⏰ 7am-1pm Mon-Sat

ARTS & CRAFTS

Bačan (3, C2)
Red-on-white embroidery is the most distinctive feature of Croatian fabric. In this little shop you can find tablecloths, shirts, napkins and blouses that will remind you of Croatia.
☎ 321 121 ⊠ Prijeko 6 ⏰ 9am-7pm Mon-Sat

Deša (3, F5)
Downstairs in Lazareti (p18), this spacious studio has a wide assortment of local crafts that includes everything from figurines to fabrics. The shop is run by an organisation designed to help Dubrovnik's women by encouraging their creative energies and economic independence.
☎ 420 145 ⊠ Lazareti ⏰ 8am-4pm Mon-Fri

Bright and early: the Morning Market at Gundulićeva Poljana

NIMBLE FINGERS

Croatian women of a certain age are as handy with a needle as they are with a rolling pin. They mend, sew, crochet, embroider and make lace. You can watch their fingers fly over cloth as they sit along the Old Harbour (3, E3). Some dress in traditional costume and all sell their wares. Don't hesitate to bargain.

Pharmacy of the Franciscan Monastery (3, B2)

Anti-wrinkle, anti-aging, anti-dryness: the creams and lotions for sale here have been fighting skin battles since the 14th century. Plus, the ingredients are derived from the purest local plant extracts.

☎ 321 411 ⊠ Placa 30 🕑 7am-8pm Mon-Fri, 7.30am-3pm Sat

CLOTHING & JEWELLERY

Jewellery Gallery Đardin (3, C3)

The contemporary jewellery here is designed by the hottest Croatian artisans, using precious and semi-precious stones with an emphasis on coral and silver. It's worth strolling through the shop for the spacey interior design alone.

☎ 324 744 ⊠ Miha Pracata 8 🕑 8am-7pm

Kadena (3, B2)

Two Zagreb designers have filled this boutique with their simple but stylish skirts, slacks, jackets and suits. Hand-crafted jewellery from Hvar Island nicely complements the fashionable look.

⊠ Celestina Medovića 2 🕑 9am-8pm

Ronchi Hats (3, D3)

The handmade hats here are extraordinary creations, full of whimsy and charm. After nearly 150 years making and selling hats in Dubrovnik, the shop is currently in the hands of designer Marina Grabovac, who learned the craft from her mother.

☎ 323 699 ⊠ Lučarića 2 🕑 9am-7pm Mon-Fri, 9am-4pm Sat

CLOTHING & SHOE SIZES

Women's Clothing

Aust/UK	8	10	12	14	16	18
Europe	36	38	40	42	44	46
Japan	5	7	9	11	13	15
USA	6	8	10	12	14	16

Women's Shoes

Aust/USA	5	6	7	8	9	10
Europe	35	36	37	38	39	40
France only	35	36	38	39	40	42
Japan	22	23	24	25	26	27
UK	3½	4½	5½	6½	7½	8½

Men's Clothing

Aust	92	96	100	104	108	112
Europe	46	48	50	52	54	56

Japan	S	M	M		L	
UK/USA	35	36	37	38	39	40

Men's Shirts (Collar Sizes)

Aust/Japan	38	39	40	41	42	43
Europe	38	39	40	41	42	43
UK/USA	15	15½	16	16½	17	17½

Men's Shoes

Aust/UK	7	8	9	10	11	12
Europe	41	42	43	44½	46	47
Japan	26	27	27½	28	29	30
USA	7½	8½	9½	10½	11½	12½

Measurements approximate only; try before you buy.

SOUNDS OF DUBROVNIK

A CD of local music can conjure up your Dubrovnik stay better than any other souvenir. If you heard a group of male voices singing in harmony, you were listening to *klapa*, traditional songs usually lamenting the homesickness of sailors. Although each region of Croatia has its own *klapa*, Dalmatian *klapa* is particularly beloved. For the best Dalmatian *klapa*, look in local shops for the *Klapi Cambi Songs of Croatia* CD. If classical music is your passion, discover Dubrovnik-born Luka Sorkočević (1734–89). His Haydn-influenced symphonies were recorded by Salzburg Hofmusic on the CPO label. For the best in local pop, try Oliver Dragojević, the enormously successful crooner from the nearby island of Korčula.

MUSIC & BOOKS

Algebra (3, C3)
Most of it is dedicated to books in Croatian but there's an excellent collection of books about Dubrovnik, Croatia and the Balkans in English. Reading up on regional history, cuisine and travel narratives is an asset to any trip.
☎ 323 217 ⊠ Placa 9
🕑 9.30am-7pm Mon-Sat

Algoritam (3, D3)
Bestsellers and classics in paperback and a selection of English magazines make this store a good stop for your basic literary needs but the selection is hardly adventurous.
☎ 322 044 ⊠ Placa 8
🕑 9am-8.30pm Mon-Fri, 9am-3pm Sat, 10am-1pm Sun

Aquarius CD Shop (3, A3)
To put a soundtrack to your Dubrovnik visit, stop here for the latest Croatian tunes as well as traditional and classical Dubrovnik music.

☎ 323 388 ⊠ Poljana Paska Miličevića 4 🕑 9am-7.30pm Mon-Sat, 9am-1pm Sun

FOOD & DRINK

Franja Coffee & Teahouse (3, C3)
Despite the name, it's not just coffee and tea for sale here. There's an excellent selection of Croatian

delicacies that includes fig brandy from Istria, olive oil from Korčula, cheese from Pag and dozens of honeys, jams, special cakes and other tasty souvenirs.
☎ 324 816 ⊠ Od Puča 9
🕑 9am-7pm Mon-Sat

Kraš (3, C3)
Satisfy your chocolate cravings here with chocolatey treasures stuffed with nuts, fruit or just more chocolate. There's also a colourful assortment of sweets to indulge your sweet tooth.
☎ 321 049
🖥 www.kras.hr
⊠ Zamanjina 2
🕑 9am-7pm Mon-Sat

Vinoteka Dubrovnik (3, D3)
After sampling some of the regional wines with dinner, you may want to bring home a bottle or two. The selection here is excellent and the prices are reasonable.
☎ 321 777 ⊠ Placa bb
🕑 10am-8pm

Sweet, succulent figs at the Morning Market (p27)

Eating

The bad news is that there's not a lot of variety on Dubrovnik menus. If you've visited the rest of the Dalmatian coast, you'll see many similarities: plenty of grilled fish and seafood, pasta, 'black' risotto made with squid ink and *brodetto* (fish stew). The good news is that the quality is fairly steady; it's difficult, although not impossible, to get a bad meal. If you eat in one of the many restaurants along Prijeko your chances of being disappointed increase dramatically. For the most part, Dubrovnik chefs are scrupulous in buying fish newly hauled from the Adriatic and preparing it carefully, usually with olive oil or butter and garlic. Meat is usually grilled, but a few places serve roast lamb or pork. There's also no shortage of pizza and it's fresh, not frozen.

PRICING INFORMATION

Prices have been climbing steadily in recent years, especially for fish and seafood, which runs from 300–400KN per kilo, depending on the type of fish and the season. Unfortunately, the Adriatic's once-teeming waters are slowly being fished out. Calamari and mussels are the cheapest seafood, while oysters and scorpion fish are among the most expensive. The price categories below are for a two-course dinner for one without wine but that may include a moderately expensive fish.

€	up to 70KN
€€	71–140KN
€€€	141–300KN
€€€€	over 300KN

OLD TOWN

Antunini (3, C2)
Adriatic €€
Even though it's on tourist-ridden Prijeko, the food in this family restaurant is good, especially the fish stew of bream and polenta. Unlike the other restaurants on this street, the interior is beautifully decorated in traditional Dubrovnik style.

☎ 321 199 ⌧ Prijeko 30 🕑 9am-1am **V**

Buffet Skola (3, C3)
Sandwiches €
For a quick bite between sightseeing spots, you can't do better. Fresh cheese, local tomatoes, local ham are some of the ingredients stuffed into the heavenly homemade bread here.

☎ 321 096 ⌧ Antuninska 1 🕑 10am-6pm **V**

Cafe Royal (3, D4)
International €€€
When nothing but white tablecloths, fine silver and polished service will do, head to the Pučić Palace hotel (p41) for this sophisticated Parisian-style restaurant. The chef ably balances creativity with tradition to create truly memorable meals and the wine list is superb.

☎ 326 200 ⌧ Pučić Palace, Od Puća 1 🕑 noon-midnight **V**

Cervantes (3, D3)
Tapas €
Noisy and convivial, there isn't much of Iberia on the menu but the prices are reasonable and you can stop in just to have a drink and snack on Croatian-style tapas.

THE BEST OF THE BEST

- Best for romance: Levanat (p34)
- Best for business: Porat (p32)
- Best seafood: Proto (p33)
- Best steaks: Domino (p31)
- Best pizza: Mea Culpa (p32)
- Best pasta: Konobo Atlantic (p34)
- Best value for money: Kamenice (p31)
- Best local scene: Lokando Peskarija (p31)
- Best for backpackers: Cervantes (p30)

☎ 321 575 ✉ Dropčeva 4a
🕑 9am-11pm 🅥

Chihuahua Cantina Mexicana (3, F2)
Mexican €

No matter how good the local cuisine is, sometimes the palate cries out for exotic spices. The tapas, fajitas and empanadas may be ersatz Mexican but it is a refreshing change from pasta, risotto and fish. The crowd is young and lively.

☎ 424 445 ✉ Hvarska 6
🕑 5-11pm 🅥

Domino (3, B4)
Meat €€

If you must have a steak fix, this large and touristy restaurant is for you. The cuts are the best in town but the other items don't offer the best value for money. It's often filled with large groups.

☎ 432 832 ✉ Od Domina 6 🕑 11am-midnight ♿

Dundo Maroje (3, D3)
Adriatic €€

This cosy restaurant has been a longtime favourite but success hasn't spoiled the good honest cooking that emphasizes fish and seafood. The owner is well connected with local wine producers; you can rely on the quality of the house wine.

☎ 321 445
✉ Kovačka
🕑 noon-11pm

Kamenice (3, D4)
Seafood €

The menu is small but the portions are huge at this animated hangout. Known for its mussels, it's often so crowded with locals at

Café Society on Placa (p8)

lunchtime you'll have to sit on the outdoor terrace. That's no hardship as you'll be looking out on one of Dubrovnik's more scenic squares.

☎ 421 499
✉ Gundulićeva Poljana 8
🕑 7am-10pm ♿

Labirint (3, E3)
International €€€

Don't expect homespun cooking here, not with specialties like ostrich with truffles and smoked salmon risotto. The modern Mediterranean decor is as inviting as the cuisine. And, after dinner you can dance it off at the Labirint disco (p38).

☎ 435 352 ✉ Svetog Dominika bb 🕑 noon-midnight 🅥

Lokando Peskarija (3, E4)
Fish & Seafood €

Located on the Old Harbour right next to the fish market,

you'll feast on the freshest catch here. Locals chow down on a hearty plate of fried sardines and finish with a *rozata Dubrovnik* (flan) for dessert. The interior is atmospheric and from the outside tables you can watch the boats come and go over a glass of good local wine.

☎ 324 750
✉ Ribarnica bb
🕑 8am-midnight

Marco Polo (3, D3)
Seafood €€

In cold weather you'll be crammed into an over-cosy dining room but in mild weather you'll be seated outside on a pleasant square. It's a dependable choice for all the best seafood dishes prepared and served in traditional Dalmatian style.

☎ 323 719
✉ Lučarića 6
🕑 10am-midnight

Tuck into grilled squid and Dalmatian vegetables

Mea Culpa (3, B3)
Pizza €

A good pizza should have the correct balance between crust and topping. Too much crust and the pie is dry; too much topping and it's a gloopy mess. The pizza chef here has perfected the winning formula, turning out pizzas big enough for at least two people from a wood-fired oven.
☎ 424 819
✉ Za Rokum 3
🕑 8am-midnight 🚼 Ⅴ

Nautika (3, A2)
International €€€€

Dining here is a dressy affair. The seafood is dressed up with ingredients like truffles, caviar and anything else that costs a fortune. The staff are dressed up in period costume. The late Pope John Paul II came once, also dressed up. The one item on the menu that's not dressed up is also, arguably, the best: oysters from the nearby Pelješac Peninsula.
☎ 442 573 🖳 www. esculap-teo.hr ✉ Brsalje 3 🕑 noon-midnight Ⅴ

Orhan (2, E5)
Adriatic €€

Overlooking a rocky cove just outside the city walls, the setting here is delightful. With waves slapping the rocks beneath you, you can dine on a full menu of fresh seafood dishes or try a lovely 'black' risotto.
☎ 414 183
✉ Od Tabakarije 1
🕑 11am-midnight

Poklisar (3, E3)
International €

There's a good assortment of styles at this casual harbourside restaurant. The salads are imaginative, the pastas are well prepared and you can sink your teeth into a steak if you like.
☎ 322 176 ✉ Ribarnica 1
🕑 11am-11pm Ⅴ

Porat (2, E5)
International €€€

Do you need money? In the Hilton Imperial Hotel (p41), this is the kind of discreetly tasteful place sure to impress potential business partners, clients and financial backers. The service is impeccable, the food cooked just so and the prices reveal you as neither cheap nor extravagant.
☎ 320 320 ✉ Hilton Imperial Hotel, Marijana Blažića 2 🕑 7am-11pm Ⅴ

Posat (3, A2)
Adriatic €€

When locals are in the mood for a special meal, especially for a romantic occasion, they come here to wine and dine in the leafy upstairs courtyard. The menu is short and concentrates on simply prepared fish.
☎ 421 194
✉ Uz Posat 1
🕑 11am-midnight

DINING DUBROVNIK STYLE

- Breakfast is eaten at home, if at all. Forget about eggs etc and settle for a bread or pastry to accompany your coffee in a café
- A 10KN cover charge is usually added to the bill
- For tipping you normally 'round up' the bill
- Fish is sold by weight; one portion is usually about 250g
- Credit cards are accepted everywhere except in the most modest establishments
- Reservations are usually not necessary except in the most upmarket places during high season

Proto (3, C3)
Seafood €€€

Under the same management as swanky Nautika, this restaurant offers simpler dishes and a more casual atmosphere. It's become a blockbuster success largely because the fish and seafood are chosen with care and expertly prepared. There's not a lot of fuss in the preparation, which allows the natural flavours to shine. Vegetarians will enjoy the wonderful *župa dubrovačka* potatoes prepared with rosemary.

☎ 323 234 🖳 www.esculap-teo.hr ✉ Široka 1 🕚 11am-11pm Ⓥ

Ragusa 2 (3, D2)
Adriatic €

It's unfortunate that this restaurant has chosen the tout mode of attracting business. It's not necessary. The good food can stand on its own. Try the Dubrovnik Plate, with local prosciutto, cheese from Pag Island and maybe a mussel or two.

☎ 321 203 ✉ Zamanjina 12 🕚 8am-1am

Restaurant Jadran (3, B3)
Croatian €€

The menu tries to offer everything to everyone and mostly succeeds. From meat to fish to vegetables, the food is fresh and unpretentious. It's also a great pleasure to eat under the Gothic arches of this former convent. There's a great deal of seating here, making it likely you'll find a table when other restaurants are full.

☎ 323 405 ✉ Poljana Paska Milčević 🕚 10am-1am ♿

Rozarij (3, D3)
Adriatic €€

Squirrelled away in a pretty little corner of Dubrovnik next to St Nicholas Church, this is a nice, quiet choice for a candlelit dinner. The shellfish risotto is outstanding but you can't go wrong whatever you choose.

☎ 321 257 ✉ Prijeko 2 🕚 11am-midnight

Shanghai (2, E5)
Chinese €€

The red decor that seems to be mandatory in all Chinese restaurants is enhanced by genuinely lovely Asian flourishes. The cuisine, while not adventurous, is thoroughly authentic, offering good versions of the world's most beloved Chinese dishes.

☎ 425 754 ✉ Branitelja Dubrovnika 🕚 5-11pm Mon, noon-11pm Tue-Sun Ⓥ

Spaghetteria Toni (3, C4)
Italian €

If you thought you knew about pasta, the chef here could teach you a trick or two. Fresh, homemade pasta combined with an assortment of imaginative fillings and sauces makes this the best pasta palace in town.

☎ 323 134 ✉ Božidarevića 14 🕚 11am-11pm Ⓥ

Tanti Gusti (3, C3)
Bakery €

Breads and cakes, pastry, tarts, rolls and biscuits; you may find yourself starting and ending your day in this immensely popular bakery.

✉ Između Polača 1 🕚 24hr

Tavern Rustica (2, F5)
Adriatic €€€

As the restaurant of the deluxe Hotel Excelsior (p41), the Tavern Rustica has to be impressive and it is. The view over the sea is breathtaking but it's the attention to authenticity that really sets this restaurant apart. The accent is on the best of Adriatic cuisine and the results are excellent.

✉ Hotel Excelsior, Frana Supila 12 🕚 7pm-1am Ⓥ 🚌 5, 8

Seafood and sea views at classy Nautika (p32)

LAPAD

Eden (2, B3)
Adriatic €€€
There's nothing particularly startling about the menu; it's got the basic risotto-pasta-grilled fish staples. What the menu lacks in originality, it makes up for in the quality of its ingredients and the scrupulous care the chef takes in letting their flavours emerge. The dining room is upstairs on a terrace verdant with plants and bushes.
☎ 435 133 ✉ Kardinala Stepinca 54 🕑 noon-midnight 🚌 5, 6, 7b, 9

Komin (2, A3)
Croatian €€
The cuisine here encompasses specialties from other regions of Croatia. The hearty baked lamb and veal makes a welcome change from the ubiquitous grilled fish that dominates other regional menus but there's a healthy sampling of marine life here if you prefer.
☎ 435 636 ✉ Iva Dulčića bb, Babin Kuk 🕑 noon-midnight Ⓥ 🚌 5

Konobo Atlantic (2, B3)
Italian €€
It's not terribly atmospheric at the outdoor tables next to a bus stop, but install yourself indoors, and you can sample superb homemade pasta like vegetarian lasagne and tagliatelle with assorted seafood sauces.
☎ 435 726 ✉ Kardinala Stepinca 42 🕑 noon-11pm Ⓥ 🚌 5, 6, 7b, 9

Levenat (2, B3)
Adriatic €€
The interior is classic and the outdoor terrace has a smashing view of the sea. The dishes are highly original (for Dubrovnik) and include such highlights as prawns with honey, fish carpaccio and rocket fried with mozzarella. The culinary feats are executed perfectly. There's no better address in Lapad.
☎ 435 352 ✉ Šetalište Nika i Meda Pucića 15 🕑 8am-midnight Ⓥ 🚌 5, 6, 7b, 9

Orsan Yacht Club (2, C3)
Adriatic €€
You would think that a yacht club would be overpriced but this restaurant offers excellent value for money and it's a most peaceful spot. The menu won't startle you with new ideas but there are a range of Dalmatian dishes from rib steak to *skampi buzara.*
☎ 435 933 🖳 www.orsan.cjb.net ✉ I. Zajca 2 🕑 8am-midnight 🚌 6, 9

Pergola (2, B3)
Adriatic €€
On a busy corner in Lapad, the outdoor terrace here is an oasis of calm in which to enjoy delicious fish and meat dishes accompanied by local wine.
☎ 436 848 ✉ Šetalište Kralja Tomislava 1 🕑 11am-1am 🚌 5, 6, 7b, 9

Restauracija Konavoka (2, B3)
Adriatic €
Near the Hotel Sumratin (p44), this restaurant has an upstairs roof terrace attractively decorated with potted plants, making it a pleasant place to hang out or enjoy a seafood meal, cheap pizza or vegetarian platter.
☎ 435 105 ✉ 38 Kralja Zvonimira 🕑 11am-midnight Ⓥ 🚌 5, 6, 7b, 9

WORTH A TRIP
Konavoski Dvori Traditional Adriatic €€
The word 'rustic' could have been coined for this restaurant in the Konavle Valley, next to a stream and a water mill. It has all the contraptions of rusticity including waitresses in traditional costume, stone walls, a blazing fireplace and a wood-fired oven. Tour groups love it but the food is good too. You can get fresh trout, home-smoked ham and the kind of mountain food that takes days to prepare.
☎ 791 039 ✉ Ljuta 🕑 11am-midnight 🚍 18km southeast of Cavtat (1, C2)

Orsan Fish €€
The simply grilled fish and seafood here are quite delicious and you're so close to the sea you could reach in and grab a fish yourself. Prices here in Zaton (1, B2) are lower than in Dubrovnik, which is why the restaurant attracts a devoted coterie of locals.
☎ 891 267 ✉ Štikovica 42, Zaton 🕑 noon-midnight 🚍 any Split-bound bus, 30 mins

Entertainment

With visitors and money flowing into Dubrovnik, the city's entertainment scene has skyrocketed in the last few years. If your interests are classical, the best time to come is during the Dubrovnik Summer Festival, when you can catch international stars as well as the best of Croatian and local performing artists. The city also has a reputable symphony orchestra, a string quartet and a woodwind trio to keep the city in music year round. Live pop music is rare as there are no arenas big enough to attract mega-bands.

Where Dubrovnik excels is in its variety of bars, nightclubs and lounges. From a romantic sunset cocktail to pulsing discos, Dubrovnik has something for everyone. Until a few years ago, Bana Josip Jelačića, near the youth hostel, was the centre of Dubrovnik's nightlife. There are still some bars there but most of the action now happens in the Old Town. A young, local crowd fills the streets of Vetranovićeva, Zamanijina and Dropćeva every weekend from around 9pm until the small hours. In Lapad, the pedestrian street Kralja Zvonimira has a number of café-bars for relaxing after a hard day at the beach.

The overall look is casual but there are a few smart places where you'll want to show off. In July and August, there's action every night but outside the main season most discos and large clubs are open weekends only.

Dalmatian folk dancing or discos

BARS & PUBS

Africa (3, C3)

If you want to meet and mix with Dubrovnik's young strivers, here's the place to do it. Beer is cheap, the ambience is cosy and the music inviting. Weekend nights are especially lively.
☎ 098 854 954
✉ Vetroniceva 3
🕑 5pm-1am

Cafe Buza (3, C5)

This ineffably romantic spot offers nothing but drinks served on outdoor tables overlooking the sea. It's just outside the city walls and you can find it by looking for the 'Cold Drinks' sign and going through a hole in the walls. Get there for the sunset.
✉ rocks outside the south walls 🕑 5pm-1am

Carpe Diem (3, B4)

It means 'seize the day' but most of the young, energetic crowd here seize the night and they don't let it go until the early hours. It's a good place to hear Croatian pop.
✉ Svetoga Josipa 13
🕑 5pm-1am

Cervantes (3, D3)

This cosy and inexpensive bar has borrowed the idea of tapas if not the actual recipes. There are small, inexpensive portions of Croatian snacks to go along with the mostly Croatian wine. It's a backpacker's favourite.
☎ 321 575
✉ Dropčeva 4a
🕑 noon-midnight 🍴

EastWest Club (2, F5)
By day, this outfit rents out beach chairs and umbrellas. When the rays lengthen, the cocktail bar opens and a smart-casual set admires the sunset over a long, cool drink.
☎ 412 220 ✉ Frana Supila bb ☽ 5pm-3am

The Gaffe Pub (3, C4)
Between this place and nearby Pub Karaka, you'll have your fill of swill. Plus, there's pub grub, Sky Sports and Irish music.
☎ 324 841
✉ Miha Pracata 4
☽ noon-midnight

Hemingway Cocktail Bar (3, D4)
Papa wouldn't have been caught dead here and nor would any self-respecting local, but the 30-page cocktail menu and comfy outdoor seating pack in visitors. This is a see-and-be-seen scene.
✉ Pred Dvorom ☽ 4pm-1am

King Richard's Pub (2, D3)
Don't take it personally, but sometimes the locals need to get away from, well, you the tourist. When they do, they leave the Old Town and come here. This café-bar couldn't be hotter, especially on Sunday afternoons. Just don't tell them we sent you.
☎ 419 577 ✉ Janjevska 1 ☽ noon-midnight 🚌 3

La Boheme (2, E5)
Chill. This café-bar is the most relaxing place in Dubrovnik to while away a summer evening. The Dubrovnik Symphony Orchestra (p39) may be giving a concert or practising here in the Crijević-Pucić Villa. Let the soft music drift through the air while you sit in a classical garden under tall trees.

SPECIAL EVENTS

With a long tradition of festivals, concerts and exhibitions, Dubrovnik is one of Croatia's most important cultural centres. The tourist office has exact dates, schedules and venues for the events below.

January
New Year's Eve Celebration – Some 30,000 people pack Placa, while ravers head to Lazareti. The most prized spot is in front of St Blaise's Church for the featured performance.

February
Feast of St Blaise – From solemn prayers and processions to dancing in the streets, celebrating Dubrovnik's patron saint is the best way to party with the locals. No sooner does the city quieten down than it gears up again for Carnival, a party that's getting wilder every year.

May
International Film Festival – It's a new festival designed to coincide with the end of the more famous festival in Cannes.

July-August
Dubrovnik Summer Festival – There are concerts and plays almost every evening in a variety of venues, including Revelin Fort and Lovrinjenac Fort, the Lazareti and a number of churches. Find out more at www.dubrovnik-festival.hr.
Karantena Festival: an international festival of alternative music, video and theatre.

September
Julian Rachlin & Friends Chamber Music Festival – The renowned Austrian violinist fell in love with Dubrovnik. His concerts are a highlight of the classical calendar each year. On the sporting calendar for this month is the *Cro Challenge*, an extreme sports competition, in which young men row, run, swim and abseil around, over and through Dubrovnik's walls.

☎ 312 688 ✉ Branitelja Dubrovnika 29
🕐 5pm-3am

Mirage (3, D4)
If Troubadour (p38) is full, a lot of the overflow comes here to loiter at one of the terrace tables. It gets particularly crowded late at night, when the DJ lets loose.
☎ 323 489 ✉ Bunićeva Poljana 3

Orka (2, C3)
Now that Croatia has cracked down on intoxicated drivers, Dubrovnik's young people prefer to stay closer to the Old Town, so Orka is not quite as popular as it once was. But if you're staying in Lapad it's certainly worthwhile checking out the scene here.
☎ 098-243-600
🖥 www.orka-du.hr
✉ Lapadska Obala 11
🚍 6, 9

Poco Loco (3, D4)
Despite the name, it's probably the least 'loco' bar in this little corner of Dubrovnik. As of now, the crowd and the music tend to be sedate but that could change at any time.
☎ 323 410 ✉ Bunićeva Poljana 5 ✗

Pub Karaka (3, C3)
The Emerald Isle is well represented here, with Irish draught beer on tap, Irish music in the evenings and a happy hour from 3pm to 7pm. You can even watch UK sports events, beamed in by satellite.
☎ 324 014 ✉ Od Polaca 7
🕐 noon-2am

Dress up to strut your stuff at swanky Labirint (p38)

Roxy (2, D4)
Near the youth hostel, this is currently the most popular of the many bars on Bana Josipa Jelačića. The crowd tends to be young and international since it's such an easy hop from the hostel.
☎ 421 754
✉ Bana Josipa Jelačića 11
🚍 1a, 1b 2, 3, 6, 7, 9

Sesame (2, E5)
Bustling and convivial, this bar-restaurant is a favourite for the local artistic crowd as well as thirsty backpackers. The small menu of reasonably priced snacks and meals is an additional draw.
☎ 412 910 ✉ Dante Alighieria bb
🕐 noon-1am ✗

CAFÉS

Café Cele (3, D3)
Locals come here to watch the pigeons and kids frolic in Luža Square and to savour the latest creations of Dubrovnik's best pastry chef. The strudels and creamy cakes are exquisite.
✉ Placa 1 🕐 9am-midnight

Café Festival (3, B3)
Placa is one of the world's most beautiful streets and this café is the best place to settle back and enjoy the view. The interior is also inviting if the weather outside isn't.
☎ 321 148
✉ Placa 28
🕐 10am-midnight

Gradska Kavana (3, D3)
You couldn't ask for a better view. To your right is Sponza Palace, to your left the Rector's Palace and in front of you St Blaise's Church. From the raised terrace of this landmark café, Dubrovnik's finest buildings frame the bustling street scene below.
✉ Pred Dvorom 3
🕐 8am-1am

Kavana Dubravka (3, A2)
Outside Pile Gate, this is
reputed to be the oldest café
in Dubrovnik. The look now is
rather modern as it has been
renovated a number of times.
It's still a great spot for coffee
and a quick snack of pastries,
small pizzas or sandwiches.
☎ 426 319 ✉ Brsalje 1
🕑 10am-midnight

Talir (3, C2)
The original art on the walls
creates a warm and inviting
atmosphere in both locations
of this café-bar. Each has
become the venue of choice
for actors and musicians
during Dubrovnik's Summer
Festival. Plus, there are
periodic exhibitions of the
work of local artists.
☎ 323 293 🖥 www.talir
-dubrovnik.hr
✉ Antuninska 5
✉ Čubranovićeva 7
🕑 9am-9pm

DANCE CLUBS & DISCOS

Capitano (3, A2)
This informal hangout really
gets going at weekends, when
the crowd spills out of the
door and fills the street. Music
is contemporary dance/pop.
✉ Između Vrta 2 🕑 5pm-
2am Wed-Sat

Exodus (2, A3)
It's big and loud and
immensely crowded on
summer nights but, if techno
is your thing, you'll want to
spend your nights here and
then crash on Copacabana
Beach.
☎ 448 355 ✉ Iva Dulčića
39 🕑 10pm-4am Thu-Sat
🚌 5, 6, 7

Labirint (3, E3)
Every night the disco in this
complex has a different
theme, from karaoke to
belly dancing, as well as
Latino nights, disco and
house tracks. It's swanky at
weekends so don your best
rags for Saturday night.
☎ 322 222
✉ Svetog Dominika 2
🕑 10pm-4am

Latino Club Fuego (2, E5)
Despite the name, you'll
find a gamut of dance music
that includes techno, rock
and pop at this disco. The
atmosphere is relaxed, with
no glowering bouncer and no
rigid dress code.
✉ Brsalje 11
🕑 10pm-4am Thu-Sat

Revelin Club (3, F2)
There's a cocktail bar on
the terrace of Revelin Fort
but the disco is down in the
dungeons. The ambience can
change from year to year of
course but, as matters now
stand, the disco tends to
attract a very young, barely
drinking-age crowd.
☎ 322 164
✉ Svetog Dominika bb
(Revelin Fort)
🕑 9pm-2am Wed-Sat

CINEMAS

Open-air cinema
You can watch movies by
starlight in two locations,
Za Rokum (3, B3) in the Old
Town and Kumičića (2, C3)
in Lapad. Films are nightly
in July and August with
screening starting after
sundown (9pm or 9.30pm).
Ask at Sloboda Cinema or
the tourist office for the
schedule.

Sloboda Cinema (3, D3)
This is the most centrally
located cinema. Posters
outside advertise the nightly
showings.
☎ 321 425
✉ Clock Tower
🕑 7pm

ROCK, JAZZ & BLUES

Troubadur (3, D4)
This place has been the
hippest bar in Dubrovnik
for years. The locals find it
expensive but fashionistas
from Zagreb have it on their
must-visit list. Marko, the
owner, is a jazz-lover and
musician. If he's not on with
his group, there's sure to be

THE THEATRICAL LIFE
Dubrovnik has a long and venerable theatrical tradition,
not least because it's the birthplace of Croatia's
proudest playwright, Marin Držić. Držić was born in
1508, and his bitingly satirical comedies earned him a
deserved comparison with Molière. His house is now
a rather uninteresting museum but the Marin Držić
Theatre in the Town Hall is a jewel. His plays are still
regularly performed there along with those of modern
playwrights such as Samuel Beckett and local artists
Feđa Šehović and Miro Gavran.

The Dubrovnik Symphony Orchestra performing at Revelin Fort

a guest group to keep things sizzling.

☎ 412 154
✉ Bunićeva 2
🕒 4pm-1am

CLASSICAL MUSIC & DANCE

Dubrovnik String Quartet
The quartet gives concerts throughout the autumn on Monday nights in St Saviour Church (p16). Look for posters around town or ask at the tourist office.

Dubrovnik Symphony Orchestra
The Dubrovnik Symphony Orchestra has a long and venerable history. Concerts are given in the atrium of the Rectors' Palace (p13), the Franciscan Monastery (p12) and at other venues around town. Details, tickets and reservations are available through the tourist office.

☎ 311 365
🖥 www.dso.com
✉ Branitelja Dubrovnika 29

Folklore Ensemble Linđo
This whirling and colourful clan of dancers performs traditional dances from all over Croatia including, of course, the Dubrovnik region. They have no permanent home but you can watch their fleet feet on Sundays at 11am in front of St Blaise's Church (p17) in May, June and September.

☎ 324 023
🖥 www.lindjo.hr
✉ M. Kaboge 12

DUBROVNIK SUMMER FESTIVAL
Ever since its inception in 1950, the Dubrovnik Summer Festival has been Croatia's most prestigious arts festival, attracting performers as diverse as the actor Daniel Day Lewis, the cellist Mstislav Rostropović, the violinist Midori and the actor Goran Višnjić. The festival opens each year on 10 July with a ceremony in front of St Blaise's Church in which the flag of Dubrovnik is raised over the Orlando Column. Until the flag is lowered on 25 August, locals and visitors flock to hear the world's finest classical musicians play in Dubrovnik's historic buildings. In addition to music, there's a full programme of theatre (in Croatian) featuring Croatia's biggest stars. Even in Croatian, seeing Lovrijenac Fort transformed into Elsinore for Shakespeare's *Hamlet* can be quite a thrill.

Sleeping

Most of Dubrovnik's hotels are gathered in Lapad, a residential neighbourhood southwest of town, in the Babin Kuk Peninsula or in Ploče, east of town by Ploče Gate. There are only a few hotels in and around the Old Town. Although Lapad seems far afield, it's actually very well connected by public transport and from there it's much easier to get to the beach. Since Babin Kuk is further out of town, the large hotels on the peninsula offer enough sports and entertainment activities to keep their guests happy. The Ploče neighbourhood is the best bet for business travellers as it is closest to town and the hotels are well equipped with conference rooms and other businesslike amenities.

Croatian hotels are graded from one to five stars according to international standards. In a five-star deluxe hotel you'll find impeccable service, lavish

All mod cons at Hotel Kompas (p43) ...

furnishings, first-rate hotel restaurants and often an indoor swimming pool or sauna in addition to gym facilities. Four-star hotels also offer an extremely high level of comfort on only a slightly less exalted level.

Three-star hotels usually offer air-conditioning, an elevator, satellite TV, telephone, minibars and hair dryers. The few two-star hotels in Dubrovnik do not have air-conditioning but the rooms are pleasant and well-kept. There are no one-star hotels in Dubrovnik.

PRICES

Most hotels in Dubrovnik are open all year but prices vary dramatically between the July-August high season and the comparative slowness of the deep winter. You'll get great deals in May and October, when prices are as much as 40% lower than in summer. Remember that you'll pay more for a sea view and a balcony in most places. The categories below indicate the cost per night of a standard double room with breakfast in high season. During high season you may be required to take half-board.

Deluxe	from €300
Top End	€200–300
Midrange	€125–200
Budget	under €125

DELUXE

Dubrovnik Palace
(2, A4)
This is the largest of Dubrovnik's five-star hotels, accommodating nearly 600 people. It manages to offer something for everyone. Families will appreciate the childcare services, there's a dozen ways for stressed-out travellers to relax and get into shape plus the business facilities are good.
☎ 430 000 ⬚ www.dubrovnikpalace.hr
✉ Masarykov put 12
🚌 4 🅿 ♿ good ⚓ ✕

Grand Villa Argentina (2, F5)
Conveniently located just outside Ploče Gate, this vast complex includes four luxury villas

... or timeless elegance and a room with a view at five-star Pucić Palace

inviting, with cheerful Mediterranean colours. Business travellers to Dubrovnik will appreciate the conference rooms, secretarial services and audo-visual equipment while leisure travellers can take advantage of the fitness room, indoor pool, and fine dining offered at the hotel's restaurant, Porat (p32).

☎ 320 320 ▢ www. dubrovnik.hilton.com ✉ Marijana Blažića 2 **P** & good ♨ ✖ Porat

Hotel Excelsior (2, F5)

This deluxe establishment offers plenty of sophisticated five-star fun. The restaurant is superb and you can work off any over-indulgence and massage your weary bones in the Wellness Centre. You could even leave richer than you arrived if you get lucky in the casino.

☎ 353 353
▢ www.hotel -excelsior.hr
✉ Frana Supila 12
🚌 5, 8 **P** ✖ Taverna Rustica (p33)

The Pucić Palace (3, D4)

Right in the heart of the Old Town, these palatial digs

and a hotel. No matter which option you choose, you'll have access to indoor and outdoor swimming pools, a sauna and fitness room and swimming from the rocks next to the hotel. All rooms and suites are stylishly furnished and the villas offer just the kind of privacy you need to hide from spies and paparazzi.

☎ 440 555 ▢ www.gva.hr ✉ Frana Supila 14 🚌 5, 8 **P** ♨ ✖

Hilton Imperial (2, E5)

Located right outside Pile Gate, the luxury Hilton Imperial is a restoration of the 19th-century Hotel

Imperial, Dubrovnik's finest establishment when the city was part of the Austrian Empire. The hotel decor is modern but warm and

Five-star comfort and sea views at the Hotel Excelsior

PRIVATE ACCOMMODATION

Private accommodation in Dubrovnik offers a more personal experience and can be an economical choice, especially for groups and families, as the cost is usually much lower than renting a few hotel rooms. You can also save money on food since apartments will include a kitchen, cutlery, dishes and a few pots and pans. Many apartments also include satellite TV but none have a telephone. Many owners expect you to stay for at least three nights and impose a surcharge of at least 30% if you fall short. You may be able to negotiate down off-season. In peak season you may be expected to stay for seven nights, especially in apartments. Private accommodation can be found when you arrive in Dubrovnik but it's better to reserve in advance, especially if you come in summer.

There are a number of agencies around the harbour that arrange private accommodation. You can also try the Atlas Travel agency (☎ 442 574; ⊠ Svetoga Đurđa 1).

have been designed and decorated to the cutting edge of fashion. It's a five-star showpiece with antiques, aromatherapy oils in the bathrooms and even a 'linen menu' which allows you to choose the quality of your Egyptian cotton towels. ☎ 326 200 ⬜ www. thepucicpalace.com ⊠ Oc Puča 1 ⊠ Cafe Royal (p30)

TOP END

Dubrovnik President (2, A3)

This is a great choice for active travellers and kids. It's near a beach shallow enough for kids to safely wade into while adults can bike, play tennis, water ski or swim in the indoor pool. Rooms are spacious and well outfitted and all have a sea view. The decor is sleekly modern and bathrooms have all the

comforts you would expect in a four-star hotel. ☎ 441 100 ⬜ www. babinkuk.com ⊠ Iva Dulčića 39 ➡ 5, 6, 7 P ♿ ✕

Hotel Uvala (2, B4)

Turkish baths, Finnish saunas, massages, spas, indoor and outdoor pools, macrobiotic food on the restaurant menu; wellness is on the way at this brightly renovated establishment. There are facilities for business travellers, sporty types, families and culture-seekers. You won't be bored. ☎ 433 580 ⬜ www. hotelimaestral.com ⊠ Masarykov Put 6 ➡ 4 P ✕

Villa Dubrovnik (3, off F5)

This is a lovely option if you're looking for a more secluded, romantic

atmosphere. It's 1.3km east from the Old Town and right above the sea with its own private rocky beach. In addition to regular buses to the centre, the hotel also runs a free boat shuttle. ☎ 422 933 ⬜ www. villal-dubrovnik.hr ⊠ Vlaha Bukovca 6 ➡ 5, 8 P ✕

Villa Wolff (3, B3)

Right next door to the Hotel Kompas, the Villa Wolff is a much more intimate establishment, offering only 15 beds in seven stylishly decorated rooms. After relaxing in your Jacuzzi, you can have a drink on the terrace overlooking the sea and sample good grilled fish in the hotel restaurant. ☎ 438 710 ⬜ www. villa-wolff.hr ⊠ Nika i Meda Pucića 1 ➡ 4 P ✕

MIDRANGE

Hotel Argosy (2, A2)

Amid the shrubs and gentle pathways on Babin Kuk, the Hotel Argosy offers a great environment for kids. There's a children's playground, a children's pool and a wide, shallow beach perfect for frolicking tots. All rooms have a view either of the sea or the greenery behind the hotel. ☎ 446 100 ⬜ www. babinkuk.com ⊠ Iva Dulčića 41 ➡ 5, 6, 7 P ♿ ✕

Hotel Komodor (2, B4)

As one of the oldest hotels in Lapad, the Komodor offers a more traditional ambience than other establishments in the neighbourhood. Still, there's no lack of modern comforts, from an outdoor swimming pool to gleaming modern bathrooms. After breakfast on the outdoor terrace, you're only steps from the sea.

☎ 433 500 ▢ www.hotelimaestral.com ✉ Masarykov Put 5 🚌 4 Ⓟ ✕

Hotel Kompas (2, B3)

This sprawling complex along the coast has an indoor and outdoor swimming pool, a sauna and an internet café. It's so close to the beach you can practically roll out of bed and into the water in a single movement.

☎ 352 000 ▢ www.hotel-kompas.hr ✉ Šetalište Kralja Zvonimira 🚌 4 ♨ ✕

Hotel Lapad (2, C3)

The hotel is a solid old limestone structure, with simple but neat and cheerful rooms. More expensive rooms with air-conditioning are available. There's no beach access but the hotel runs a daily boat to a remote beach near Zaton for a small charge.

☎ 432 922 ▢ www.hotel-lapad.hr ✉ Lapadska Obala 37 🚌 6, 9 Ⓟ

Hotel Minčeta (2, A2)

From baking in the sun to learning some Croatian, there's a lot to do at this three-star hotel in Babin Kuk. It's huge and modern, with a large outdoor swimming pool and a full menu of sports activities. It also offers an all-inclusive programme for better budgetary control.

☎ 447 100 ▢ www.

babinkuk.com ✉ Iva Dulčića 18 🚌 5, 6, 7 Ⓟ ♨ ✕

Hotel Perla (2, B3)

This new entry on the hotel scene is on one of Lapad's livelier streets but the rooms are set far enough back from the street to preserve tranquillity. Rooms are equipped with air-conditioning, satellite TV, internet and minibars. The front rooms have attractive terraces.

☎ 438 244 ▢ www.perla-dubrovnik.com ✉ Kralja Zvonimira bb 🚌 4 ✕ Agona

Hotel Petka (2, C3)

This big, modern hotel, opposite the Jadrolinija ferry dock, has 104 rooms, each with TV, phone and minibar. It would not be your ideal honeymoon hotel but the

amenities are fine and the location is great if you need to catch an early-morning ferry.

☎ 410 500 ▢ www.hotelpetka.com ✉ Obala Stjepana Radića 38 🚌 1a, 1b, 3, 7, 8 Ⓟ ✕

Hotel Splendid (2, A3)

This resort hotel has 59 comfortable rooms, each with a terrace overlooking the sea. Amenities such as air-conditioning, satellite TV, direct dial phones and minibars have earned it three-star status. You can zip into town from a nearby bus stop and trot across the street to a small cove.

☎ 437 304 ▢ www.hotelimaestral.hr ✉ Masarykov Put 10 🚌 4 Ⓟ ✕

Hotel Stari Grad (3, C2)

Staying in the heart of the Old Town in a lovingly

Try to bag one of the eight rooms at the delightful Hotel Stari Grad

restored stone building is a delightful experience. There are only eight rooms, each one furnished with taste and a sense of comfort. From the rooftop terrace, you have a marvellous view over the town. Prices stay the same all year.

☎ 322 244 ⌨ www.hotelstarigrad.com ✉ Od Sigurate 4 ✗

Hotel Zagreb (2, B3)
This is under the same ownership as the Hotel Sumratin, but the Hotel Zagreb has recently been overhauled and is now a three-star hotel with air-conditioning, shiny new bathrooms and other accoutrements. It's in a restored 19th-century building with more character than you usually find along the coast. The ceilings are high and the hotel is behind a shady garden.

☎ 436 146 ⌨ www.hotels-sumratin.com ✉ Šetalište Kralja Zvonimira 27 🚌 5, 6, 7b, 9 Ⓟ

BUDGET

Apartments van Bloemen (4, E4)
This is the most personal and original accommodation, with a great location in the Old Town. All four apartments are beautifully decorated with original art created or amassed by owner Sheila van Bloemen. Three of the four rooms sleep three people comfortably and all are quiet.

☎ 323 433, 091 33 24 106 ⌨ www.karmendu.tk ✉ Bandureva 1

Hotel Adriatic (2, B3)
For a two-star hotel, the Adriatic offers good value for money. Front rooms are more expensive and overlook the sea but could be noisy. Rooms in the rear overlook a pine grove. Everything is clean, modern and well maintained and the hotel is just across from the beach, with a panoply of water sports.

☎ 437 302 ⌨ www.hotelimaestral.com ✉ Masarykov Put 9 🚌 4 Ⓟ ♿

Hotel Sumratin (2, B3)
It's one of the increasingly rare two-star hotels in Dubrovnik but offers good value for money. No one would accuse the rooms of being over-decorated but they are quite adequate and

there's a terrace. Plus, the hotel is well located near the shops of Lapad and the beach.

☎ 436 333 ⌨ www.hotels-sumratin.com ✉ Kralja Zvonimira 31 🚌 5, 6, 7b, 9 Ⓟ

Vila Micika (2, B3)
Under the same management as the Orsan Yacht Club restaurant (p34), this is a simple, well-run establishment. The rooms have the necessities but offer few decorative flourishes. Still, there's a pleasant outdoor terrace and it's only 200m to the Lapad beaches.

☎ 437 332 ⌨ www.vilamicika.hr ✉ Mata Vodapica 10 🚌 5, 6, 7b, 9 Ⓟ

Cosy and characterful décor at the Apartments van Bloemen

About Dubrovnik

HISTORY

The story of Dubrovnik begins with the 7th-century onslaught of barbarians that wiped out the Roman city of Epidaurum (site of present-day Cavtat). The residents fled to the safest place they could find, which was a rocky islet separated from the mainland by a narrow channel.

Recent excavations reveal that the islet was probably inhabited at the time but the new settlers increased the population and named their new sanctuary Laus, Greek for 'rock'. Eventually it became known as Rausa, Ragusa and Ragusium. This inaccessible settlement was located around the southern walls of present-day Dubrovnik.

Building walls was a matter of pressing urgency at the time, when barbarian invasions were a constant threat; it appears that the city was well fortified by the 9th century, when it resisted a Saracen siege for 15 months.

The town had help in the form of the powerful Byzantine Empire, however, under whose protection Ragusa remained from the 7th to the 12th century. Meanwhile, another settlement emerged on the mainland, stretching from Zaton in the north to Cavtat in the south. This settlement became known as Dubrovnik, named after the *dubrava* (holm-oak) that carpeted the region. The two settlements merged in the 12th century, and the channel that separated them was paved over to become Placa.

By the end of the 12th century Dubrovnik had become an important trading centre on the coast, providing an important link between the Mediterranean and Balkan states. From the hinterlands, cattle and dairy products, wax, honey, timber, coal, silver, lead, copper and slaves were exported, along with Dubrovnik products such as salt, cloth, wine, oil and fish.

Towering Lovrijenac Fort (p19)

The Gothic Clock Tower (p9) on Placa

As the city grew increasingly prosperous it posed a threat to the other major commercial interest in the Adriatic – Venice. Dubrovnik came under Venetian authority in 1205 and remained under its control for 150 years. Despite accepting governance from Venice, the city continued to establish its own independent commercial relations and finally broke away from Venetian control in 1358. Although the city thereafter acknowledged the authority of the Croatian-Hungarian kings and paid them tribute, it was largely left alone to do what it did best – make money.

By the 15th century 'Respublica Ragusina' (the Republic of Ragusa) had extended its borders to include the entire coastal belt from Ston to Cavtat, having previously acquired Lastovo Island, the Pelješac Peninsula and Mljet Island. It was now a force to be reckoned with. The city turned towards sea trade and established a fleet of its own ships, which were dispatched to Egypt, Syria, Sicily, Spain, France and later Turkey. Through canny diplomacy the city maintained good relations with everyone – even the Ottoman Empire, to which Dubrovnik began paying tribute in the 16th century.

Dubrovnik's 'Golden Age' continued until the beginning of the 17th century, when England and Holland came on the scene as rival maritime powers. The 1667 earthquake (p15) was the *coup de grace* for Dubrovnik's rule. To counter the rise of Turkish power, Dubrovnik accepted Austrian sovereignty and then in 1806 accepted French sovereignty when Napoleon Bonaparte announced the end of the republic. The Vienna Congress of 1815 ceded Dubrovnik to Austria. The city maintained its

DID YOU KNOW...

- The word 'argosy' is derived from 'Ragusa'
- Ragusa once had 85 consulates lodged in Mediterranean ports
- Columbus had two Ragusan mariners aboard in 1492 when he landed in America
- The slave trade was abolished in Ragusa in 1418
- Ragusa opened its first hospital in 1347 and offered health care to all its citizens
- All male citizens of Ragusa received free education
- Ragusa installed a sewage system in 1296, one of the earliest in Europe

shipping but succumbed to social disintegration. It remained a part of the Austro-Hungarian Empire until 1918 and then slowly began to develop its tourist industry. The town awed luminaries such as Lord Byron, George Bernard Shaw and Agatha Christie and Dubrovnik became a major tourist centre in postwar Yugoslavia.

In December 1991, Serbian artillery launched an attack on Dubrovnik. As the world watched in horror, the city was pummelled with some 2000 shells in 1991 and 1992. Tourism declined precipitously and residents were left feeling isolated and abandoned. The resurgence of the city has been nothing less than astonishing as Dubrovnik has taken its place among the world's leading destinations.

Statue of Miho Pracat (p13)

ENVIRONMENT

The link between a healthy environment and a healthy tourist business is not lost on Dubrovnik's city planners, who have struggled to ensure clean air and water. The surrounding water is crystal-clean and the beaches in front of the Hotel President and Neptun have been awarded coveted Blue Flag status. The city's main environmental problem is heavy traffic, especially in high season and despite an excellent public transport system.

GOVERNMENT & POLITICS

Dubrovnik's mayor is the former teacher Dubravka Šuica, of Croatia's nationalist HDZ party. Acknowledging that the city's wellbeing depends on tourism, Mayor Šuica has been proactive in improving its infrastructure. After overseeing the expansion of the fleet of city buses and the construction of a new bus station, she has lent her support to an as-yet-unrealised plan to build a megayacht facility in Gruž. Nevertheless, her relationship with the Croatian government in Zagreb has been prickly. She has turned to UNESCO for funds to safeguard Dubrovnik's ancient monuments, claiming that the national government in Zagreb has been too stingy with development funds. Zagreb, in turn, has accused her of wasting the funds she has received. Part of the problem is bureaucratic: Dubrovnik does not have much autonomy in determining its priorities and must turn to the county and the central government in developing its projects.

THE RECONSTRUCTION OF DUBROVNIK

After the smoke cleared in 1992, one of the first and most urgent problems was repairing the city's tiled roofs in order to prevent water damage from rainfall. The rosy terracotta tiles that had topped all of Dubrovnik's buildings were originally produced in a nearby tile factory that had long since closed. Replacements of the same colour proved impossible to find. Eventually the city ordered new tiles from France and northern Croatia, scattering them randomly to make the different colours less obvious. A walk around the walls reveals the patchwork of colours that should, one day, weather into one.

The restorers faced a similar problem in repairing the city's buildings and monuments, built in and carved from fine white limestone. The original stone came from nearby Vrnik, off the island of Korčula, but the quarries fell into disuse and are now capable of producing only small amounts of stone. The restorers decided to use Vrnik stone in the most visible places and use stone from the island of Brač to make repairs in less visible places.

Capital detail at the Rector's Palace (p13)

ECONOMY

Tourism has been very, very good to Dubrovnik even though visitor numbers have yet to reach pre-war levels. Money is pouring into the city; some of it even manages to fill the pockets of residents as opposed to those of the big businesses that run the luxury hotels and restaurants. In addition to tourism-related employment, many locals double up with friends or family in the high season and rent out their room or apartment. This provides a welcome supplement to the generally low wages and modest pensions that Croatians live on. The biggest challenge for locals is the spiralling cost of real estate, which prices local families out of the market.

SOCIETY & CULTURE

The shelling of 1991 sorely tested Dubrovnik's long history of tolerance towards ethnic minorities. Many residents speak with bitterness about former Serb friends who, they feel, were aware that the city was about to be attacked yet said nothing. Longstanding Serb families that withstood the bombing along with others are accepted but the idea of 'forgive and forget' is a long way from being applied to anyone from Serbia and Montenegro.

ARTS
Architecture

Within the harmony and modesty that characterise Dubrovnik's cityscape lies a range of styles. The Gothic style is beautifully represented in the cloister of the Franciscan Monastery (p12) and in the statue of the *Pietà* over the

The atrium of the Rector's Palace (p13) is used for concerts in the Summer Festival

entrance. Notice also the Gothic windows on the main façade of the Rector's Palace (p13).

At the height of the Ragusa Republic, the city imported the finest architects from Italy. Often local builders, still infatuated with the Gothic style, carried out their Renaissance designs. This fascinating transitional style can be seen in the cloister of the Dominican Monastery (p11), which has Renaissance arches with Gothic tracery. The upper floors of Sponza Palace (p8) are another Gothic-Renaissance blend. The most influential of the Italian Renaissance architects was Michelozzo Michelozzi (1396–1472), a Florentine, who had a hand in designing the Rector's Palace and the Minčeta Tower (p10).

When the beautifully ornamented Renaissance buildings were lost in the earthquake of 1667 the city was rebuilt in a much simpler style. First, money was tight and, second, the ruling aristocracy decided to play down the economic inequalities within the city by erecting less showy buildings. A succession of Italian architects brought the Roman baroque style that dominates the town centre today.

Literature

The delicious satires of Marin Držić (p38), which poke fun at pompous nobility, have made him enduringly popular. His comic play *Dundo Maroje* is frequently performed at festivals. He was followed by the poet Ivan Gundulić (1589–1638), another towering figure whose powerful verses extolling liberty were put to work in support of Croatia's independence drive in 1991. His epic poem *Osman* is a masterpiece of Renaissance literature and his play, *Dubravka*, celebrates Ragusan autonomy.

Painting

More than buildings were lost in the Dubrovnik earthquake of 1667; almost all the work of the Dubrovnik school of painting that flourished in the 15th and 16th centuries went up in flames. The few surviving works testify to the high quality of the city's art. A few fine examples of Renaissance painting by Lovro Dobričević (1420–78) are preserved in the Dominican Monastery (p11) and the Franciscan Monastery (p12) but the greatest painter of the period was probably Nikola Božidarević, whose lovely polyptychs are on display in the Dominican Monastery.

Even with its greatest treasures destroyed, Dubrovnik continued to inspire artists. Born in nearby Cavtat (p25), Vlaho Bukovac (1855–1922) became one of Croatia's most important modern painters. After studying at the Ecole des Beaux Arts in Paris, Bukovac flirted with impressionism before settling into his own style. He's best known for his 400 portraits, which brought him recognition in Paris, Zagreb and Prague as well as in Dubrovnik.

Dubrovnik's major artist of the postwar period was Ivo Dulčić (1916–75) whose paintings are marked by exhuberant colours and spiritual themes. Unlike Bukovac, Dulčić chose subjects from Dubrovnik for his landscapes and portraits. On the contemporary scene, look for works by Duro Pulitika (1922–) whose paintings of local scenes are available in galleries around town.

A medieval gem at the Franciscan Monastery (p12)

Directory

ARRIVAL & DEPARTURE
Air
ČILIPI INTERNATIONAL AIRPORT
Information
Flight Information ☎ 773 377
Information Online 🖳 www.airport-dubrovnik.hr

Airport Access
Čilipi airport (2, F6) is 24km southeast of Dubrovnik. The Croatia Airlines airport buses (30KN) leave from the main bus station (2, C2) 1½ hours before flight times and collect passengers from the airport after flights on Croatia Airlines and its partners. A taxi costs about 220KN and takes about 30 minutes.

Bus
The main **bus station** (2, C2; ☎ 060-30 50 70; www.libertasdubrovnik.com) is at Obala Pape Ivana Pavla II. From here buses go to all major Croatian cities as well as to Mostar, Ljubljana, Sarajevo, Frankfurt, Munich, Trieste, Ulcinj, Skopje and Zurich.

Boat
Jadrolinija (2, C3; ☎ 418 000; www.jadrolinija.hr; Gruž) runs ferries all year between Bari and Dubrovnik as well as the coastal ferry north to Hvar, Split and Rijeka.

Travel Documents
PASSPORT & VISAS
Most visitors (from North America, Europe, Australia and New Zealand) only need a passport; EU residents can enter with a national ID card. Citizens of the EU, USA, Canada, Australia, New Zealand, Israel, Ireland, Singapore and the UK do not need a visa for stays of up to 90 days. South Africans must apply for a 90-day visa in Pretoria. Contact any Croatian embassy, consulate or travel agency abroad for information.

Croatian authorities require foreigners to register with local police when they arrive in a new area of the country, but this is a routine matter normally handled by the hotel or proprietor of an apartment. This is why they need to take your passport away for the night.

Customs & Duty Free
The import or export of kuna, the national currency, is limited to 15,000KN per person. Camping gear, boats and electronic equipment should be declared upon entering the country.

Travellers who spend more than 500KN in one store are entitled to a refund of the value-added tax (VAT), which is equivalent to 22% of the purchase price. For you to claim the refund, the shopkeeper must fill out the Poreski ček (required form), which you must present to the customs office upon leaving the country. Mail a stamped copy to the store, which will then credit your credit card with the appropriate sum.

Left Luggage
There is a left-luggage facility at the bus station (2, C2). It costs 10KN per day and is open from 4.30am to 10.30pm.

GETTING AROUND
Bus
The Old Town is a pedestrian area well connected by buses to Lapad and Babin Kuk. Buses from the Old Town leave from Pile Gate. They begin running at about 5am and pick up their last passengers around midnight. The fare is 10KN if you buy from the driver but only 8KN if you buy from a kiosk, or *tisak*. In this book, the bus route is noted after the 🚌 symbol. Timetables are posted at bus stops and buses tend to run on time. Bus routes and timetables are also set out in *Dubrovnik Riviera*, a free guide available from the tourist office, travel agencies and many hotels.

Taxi
Taxis are widely available and useful for getting to the airport. The flag fall is 25KN

and the charge is 7KN per kilometre. The most useful taxi stations are at Pile Gate (3, C2), Ploče Gate (3, E2), Jadrolinija Harbour (2, C3) and Lapad Post Office (2, B3). You can call for a taxi on ☎ 970.

Car & Motorcycle
On a short trip to Dubrovnik, you're unlikely to need your own wheels, and the traffic congestion (not to mention its environmental impact) will not make driving here a pleasant experience. However, if you do need to hire a vehicle, you could try:
Budget (3, D4; ☎ 091 201 46 38; S Radića 24)
Gulliver (2, C3; ☎ 448 296; S Radića 31)
Hertz (2, F5; ☎ 425 000; F Supila 5)

Parking
The Old Town is pedestrian only but you can park at Pile Gate (3, B2), north of the city walls (3, D2; 5KN/hr) or at Gruž harbour (2, C3; 5KN/40K per hour/day). All the car parks are open 24 hours. Should you be tempted to park illegally, remember that the tow-away service is also open 24 hours.

Petrol Stations
Convenient petrol stations include:
Lapad (2, D4; ☎ 357 366; Starčevića 76; ⏱ 7am-9pm)
Grad (2, D4; ☎ 425 151; V Nazora 2; ⏱ 6am-10pm)
Orsan (2, C3; ☎ 435 969; I Zajca 2; ⏱ 6am-10pm)

PRACTICALITIES
Business Hours
Usual office hours are from 8am to 4pm Monday to Friday. Banking and post office hours are 7.30am to 7pm on weekdays and 8am to noon on Saturday. Many shops are open 8am to 7pm on weekdays and until 2pm on Saturday. Shops are open longer in the Old Town, often seven days a week.

Restaurants are open long hours, often from noon to midnight, with Sunday closings out of peak season. Cafés are usually open daily from 10am to midnight, and bars from 5pm to 1am. Cybercafés usually open seven days a week. Opening hours of famous churches are indicated in this book; smaller churches are usually open in the morning for an hour or so before and after mass, as well as late afternoon.

Climate & When to Go
Dubrovnik's peak season is in July and August. The Dubrovnik Summer Festival (p39) is in full swing and the city is full of concerts and events. It can be uncomfortably crowded and hot, however. Accommodation is scarce and expensive during this period and it is imperative to reserve in advance. May, June, September and October are the best months to visit; the sea and air are warm, there's still plenty to do and you get a break on hotel prices. November to March is the low season but there are some great local festivals such as Carnival and the Feast of St Blaise (p17).

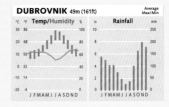

Consulates & Embassies
British Consulate (3, D4; ☎ 324 597; Bunićeva Poljana 3)

Croatian embassies and consulates abroad:
Australia (☎ 02-6286 6988; 14 Jindalee Cres, O'Malley, ACT 2601)
Canada (☎ 613-562 7820; 229 Chapel St, Ottawa, Ontario K1N 7Y6)
France (☎ 01 5370 0287; 2 rue de Lubeck, Paris)

Germany (Berlin ☎ 030-219 15 514; Ahornstrasse 4, 10787; Bonn ☎ 022-895 29 20; Rolandstraße 52, 53179)

Ireland (☎ 1 4767 181; Adelaide Chambers, Peter St, Dublin)

Netherlands (☎ 70 362 36 38; Amaliastraat 16, The Hague)

New Zealand (☎ 09-836 5581; 131 Lincoln Rd, Henderson, Auckland)

South Africa (☎ 012-342 1206; 1160 Church St, 0083 Colbyn, Pretoria)

UK (☎ 020-7387 2022; 21 Conway St, London W1P 5HL)

USA (☎ 202-588 5899; www.croatiaemb. org; 2343 Massachusetts Ave NW, Washington, DC 20008)

Disabled Travellers

Dubrovnik is extremely difficult to navigate for disabled travellers. Access to museums nearly always involves steps and the streets are not smooth. The situation is easier in restaurants in the Old Town since, in most cases, you can eat outside. With the exception of the few noted in this book, hotels have given little thought to facilities for the disabled.

Discounts

Students, children and senior citizens are entitled to discounts at most sights but not on public transport. From November to February, the tourist office distributes a free Dubrovnik Card to anyone who stays at least two nights in a hotel or private accommodation. This gives free entrance to many cultural events as well as discounts in restaurants, galleries, museums, nightclubs, car rentals and a host of other places.

STUDENT & YOUTH CARDS

Although any proof of attendance at an educational institution is acceptable, students should get an International Student Identity Card (ISIC), which is the best international proof of student status.

People under the age of 26 who are not students qualify for the International Youth Travel Card (IYTC). Applicants must present proof of age (a copy of your birth certificate, passport or driving licence), a US$22 fee, and one passport-size photo. The card, valid for one year from the date of issue, also comes with a travel handbook.

Electricity

Voltage	220V
Frequency	50Hz
Cycle	AC
Plugs	two round pins

Emergencies

Dubrovnik is largely calm and safe; there is no reason to fear anything other than the occasional pickpocket.

Ambulance ☎ 94
Fire ☎ 93
Emergency Police ☎ 92
District Police ☎ 443 333

Fitness

To burn off all the wonderful food you'll be eating in Dubrovnik you can head to the gym. The fitness rooms in some hotels are open to the public for a small fee. Try the Dubrovnik President (p42), the Hotel Uvala (p42), Hotel Kompas (p43), or Hotel Adriatic (p44).

Gay & Lesbian Travellers

Dubrovnik's beauty and reputation for tolerance has made it a popular destination for gay and lesbian travellers. Although there is no gay scene as such, gays and lesbians will feel comfortable in Dubrovnik's bars and clubs. Same-sex displays of affection should be discreet however. By far the best place to meet other like-minded travellers is on Lokrum Island (p24). The naturist beach (look for the 'FKK' sign) has become a popular meeting place for gays. For up to date information, check out www.touristinfo.gay.hr.

Health
PRECAUTIONS
Dubrovnik is a healthy and clean place. The tap water is drinkable, the food well prepared and hygienic matters are taken seriously. No particular vaccinations are necessary to enter Croatia. Your main problem is likely to be sunburn.

MEDICAL SERVICES
Good healthcare is readily available and for minor illnesses pharmacists can give valuable advice and sell over-the-counter medication. They can also advise when more specialised help is required and point you in the right direction. For EU citizens, an EHIC card, available by application from post offices in the UK or health centres in Europe, covers you for most emergency medical care. Citizens of other countries should check whether there is a reciprocal arrangement for free medical care between their country and Croatia.

Travel insurance is advisable to cover any medical treatment you may need while in Dubrovnik. Consider a policy that covers you for the worst possible scenario, such as an accident requiring an emergency flight home. Hospitals with 24hr accident and emergency departments include the **General Hospital** (2, B4; ☎ 431 777; Dr. Roka Mišetića).

DENTAL SERVICES
If you chip a tooth or require emergency treatment, head to the dental station at the hospital (2, B4; ☎ 412 433; Branitelja Dubrovnika 45; ⏱ 8am-6pm Mon-Fri).

PHARMACIES
Pharmacies are generally open from 7am to 8pm Monday to Friday and 7am to 3pm Saturday. Try:
Gruž (3, C3; ☎ 418 990; Pape Pavla Ivana II)

Kod Zvonika (3, D3; ☎ 321 133; Placa) Alternates 24-hr service with Gruž (below)
Ruskovič Merčep (2, B3; Kardinala Stepinca 1d)

Holidays

1 January	New Year's Day
6 January	Epiphany
March/April	Easter Monday
1 May	Labour Day
10 June	Corpus Christi
Day of Antifascist Resistance	22 June – marks the outbreak of resistance in 1941
25 June	National Day
5 August	Victory Day & National Thanksgiving Day
15 August	Feast of the Assumption
8 October	Independence Day
1 November	All Saints' Day
Christmas	25 & 26 December

Internet
Croatians are comfortable on the internet, especially the younger generation, but global ISPs do not have dial-up nodes in town. Most people subscribe through a local provider. You can get wireless internet access at the Grand Villa Argentina (p41) or Troubadur café (p38); the charge is 60KN per hour.

INTERNET CAFÉS
Dubrovnik Internet Centar (2, E5; ☎ 311 017; Branitelja Dubrovnika 7; per hr 20KN; 8am-midnight)
Holobit (2, B3; ☎ 352 121; Hotel Kompas; Kralja Zvonimira 56; 9am-midnight)

USEFUL WEBSITES
The Lonely Planet website (www.lonelyplanet.com) offers a speedy link to websites for Dubrovnik and Croatia. Others to try include the Dubrovnik tourist office at www.tzdubrovnik.hr.

WIRELESS ACCESS

Accessing the internet from your laptop is a convenient option in Dubrovnik. Mobile access is provided by T-com (www.t-mobile.hr) and is available at the airport, the ACI Marina, the Grand Villa Argentina Hotel (p41) and Café Troubadur (p38).

Lost Property

If you lose something on the city buses call ☎ 357 020. For property lost on the ferry call ☎ 418 000.

Metric System

Metric measures are used in Croatia and Croatians use commas in decimals, and points to indicate thousands.

TEMPERATURE

$°C = (°F - 32) ÷ 1.8$
$°F = (°C × 1.8) + 32$

DISTANCE

1in = 2.54cm
1cm = 0.39in
1m = 3.3ft = 1.1yd
1ft = 0.3m
1km = 0.62 miles
1 mile = 1.6km

WEIGHT

1kg = 2.2lb
1lb = 0.45kg
1g = 0.04oz
1oz = 28g

VOLUME

1L= 0.26 US gallons
1 US gallon = 3.8L
1L = 0.22 imperial gallons
1 imperial gallon = 4.55L

Money
CURRENCY

Commonly circulated banknotes come in denominations of 500, 200, 100, 50, 20, 10 and 5 kuna. Each kuna is divided into 100 lipa. You'll find silver-coloured 50- and 20-lipa coins, and bronze-coloured 10-lipa coins.

The kuna has a fixed exchange rate tied to the euro. To amass hard currency, the Croatian government makes the kuna more expensive in summer, when tourists visit. You'll get the best exchange rate from mid-September to mid-June. Otherwise, the rate varies little from year to year. Accommodation and international boat fares are priced in euros, although you can pay in kuna or euros. Most shops, restaurants and private accommodation accept payment in euros, although you won't get the best exchange rate.

CHANGING & TRANSFERRING MONEY

ATMs, which accept all major credit and debit cards, are in every neighbourhood. Travellers cheques and currency can be exchanged at larger hotels, banks and post offices.

CREDIT CARDS

Major credit cards are accepted in all hotels and most restaurants and shops but not in private accommodation. To report a lost or stolen credit card, call:
Amex 0800 220 111 4920 507
Diners Club 01 492 0507
Eurocard/MasterCard 00-1-636 722 7111
Visa 00-1-410 581 9994

EXCHANGE RATES

For current exchange rates see www.xe.com.

Australia	A$1	4.6KN
Canada	C$1	5.3KN
Euro zone	€1	7.3KN
Hungary	100Ft	2.9KN
Japan	¥100	5.3KN
New Zealand	NZ$1	4.1KN
Slovenia	1SIT	0.03KN
UK	UK£1	10.8KN
USA	US$1	6.1KN

Newspapers & Magazines

Every visitor should pick up a copy of *Dubrovnik Riviera*, a monthly booklet which has bus and boat timetables, restaurants, hotels, events, entertainment venues and dozens of other helpful listings. English-language newspapers and magazines are for sale on a number of newsstands.

Photography & Video

Colour-print film produced by Kodak and Fuji is widely available in photographic shops and tourist outlets. It's fairly expensive in Dubrovnik, so stock up before you arrive. If you choose to develop your photos here, remember that the standard size for prints is only 9cm x 13cm. Memory cards for your digital camera are easy to find and cybercafés will download your photos onto a CD for a reasonable fee.

Be careful about buying a video cassette souvenir here; the cassettes are in PAL format and must be played on a compatible VCR. DVDs are formatted in Zone 2, which is incompatible with Zone 1 players in the US and Canada.

Post

HPT Hrvatska is the national postal service and it's reliable. If you want to avoid a trip to the post office and just want to send a few postcards, you can buy *pismo* (stamps) at any *tisak* (newsstand) and drop your mail into any of the yellow postboxes on the street. It takes anything from five days (Europe) to two weeks (North America and Australia) for a card or letter to arrive at its destination.

Domestic mail costs 2.80KN for up to 20g, and 5KN for up to 100g. Postcards are 1.80KN. For international mail, the base rate is 3.60KN for a postcard, 7.20KN for a letter up to 20g, and 15KN for a letter up to 100g. Then, add on the airmail charge for every 10g: 1KN for Europe, 1.50KN for North America, 1.60KN for Africa and Asia, and 2KN for Australia.

Branch Post Office (2, E5; Branitelja Dubrovnika 2)
Lapad Post Office (2, B3; Kralja Zvonimira 21)
Main Post Office (3, B3; Široka & Od Puča)

Radio

The two government-owned radio stations are HRT1 and HRT2. HRT1 broadcasts a daily news programme in English and HRT2 provides traffic reports daily in English during July and August. In addition there are numerous private radio stations that broadcast nationally and locally.

Solo Travellers

The joy of travelling solo is that it is a compromise-free trip. You do what you want when you want to do it, but you will pay for the privilege. Very few hotels, guest houses or private rooms have special rates for singles, although you may be able to knock a few kuna off the double-room price if you visit out of season.

Telephone
COUNTRY & CITY CODES

To call Croatia from abroad, dial your international access code, then ☎ 385 (the country code for Croatia), then the area code (*without* the initial zero) and the local number. To call within Croatia, start with the area code (*with* the initial zero). Phone numbers with the prefix ☎ 060 are free and phone numbers that begin with ☎ 09 are mobile (cellular) phone numbers, which are billed at a much higher rate than regular numbers (reckon on about 2KN per minute).

PHONECARDS

There are few coin-operated phones, so you'll need a phonecard to use public telephones. These can be purchased at any post office and most tobacco shops and newspaper kiosks (*tisak*). Many new phone boxes are equipped with a button with a flag (top left). Press the button and you get instructions in English. If you don't have a phonecard you can call from a post office.

MOBILE PHONES

Croatia uses GSM 900/1800, which is compatible with the rest of Europe and Australia but not with the North American GSM 1900 system. If you have a GSM phone, you can buy a simcard for about 300KN, which includes 30 minutes of connection time. If you don't have a GSM phone and want the convenience of a mobile phone, you can buy a packet (mobile and phonecard) at any telecom shop for about 700KN, which includes 30 minutes of connection time.

USEFUL PHONE NUMBERS

Local Directory Inquiries ☎ 988
International Direct Dial Code ☎ 00
International Directory Inquiries ☎ 902
International Operator ☎ 902
Reverse-Charge (collect) ☎ 981

Television

There are three national TV networks: the government-owned HRT, and the privately owned Nova and RTL. HRT turns a handsome profit on a schedule of game shows, variety shows and sitcoms. Nova and RTL entered the arena within the last few years amid high hopes for improving Croatia's TV landscape but they have seen their viewers and profits decline dramatically as each searches for a winning format. Currently, RTL's most popular show is a talk show hosted by former pop-star Sanja Donežal. The good news for travellers is that there is bound to be a movie every night on one channel or another, and it's likely to be in English with subtitles. Satellite TV is installed in nearly all hotels and many privately rented apartments.

Time

Croatia is on Central European Time (GMT/UTC plus one hour). Daylight saving comes into effect at the end of March, when clocks are turned forward an hour. At the end of October they're turned back an hour.

Tipping

Tipping is rarely practised. In restaurants, it's customary to 'round up' the bill and it's appropriate to tip hotel reception staff if they have provided extraordinary service. Taxi drivers are not tipped.

Toilets

The most comfortable option is to duck into the nearest hotel to use the WC in the lobby. There's usually no problem using the toilets in a bar or café either. There are no public toilets in the Old Town but there are public toilets just outside on Frana Supila (3, F2) and on Iza Grada (3, F1). The price is 5KN.

Tourist Information

The **Dubrovnik Tourist Office** (☎ 323 887; www.tzdubrovnik.hr) is extremely helpful, publishing the indispensable *Dubrovnik Riviera* welcome booklet as well as flyers highlighting monthly events. Their offices *(Turisticka Zajednica)* are at:

Bus Station (2, C2; ☎ 417 851; Obala Pape Ivana Pavla II 44a; ☽ 8am-8pm)
Gruž (2, C3; ☎ 417 983; Obala S. Radića 27; ☽ 8am-8pm)
Lapad (2, B3; ☎ 437 460; Kralja Tomislava Shopping Centre ☽ 8am-8pm)
Pile (2, E5; ☎ 427 591; Braniteljа Dubrovnika 7; ☽ 8am-8pm)
Placa (3, C3; ☎ 321 561; Miha Pracata bb; ☽ 8am-10pm)

Women Travellers

The chivalrous attitude that makes it easy for women to visit Dubrovnik can pose an obstacle for women trying to be taken seriously in business or a profession. You'll notice many women in low-status positions and few in leadership roles. Nevertheless, Dubrovnik is a safe environment for women travellers.

LANGUAGE

Croatian is the official language of Dubrovnik but English, Italian and German are also widely spoken. Lonely Planet's Croatian phrasebook, with a 2000-word dictionary, is an invaluable aid to communicating with the city's residents in their own language.

PRONUNCIATION

Croatian is written in the Roman alphabet (unlike Serbian, which uses both the Cyrillic and Roman alphabets) and many letters are pronounced as in English. The following outlines some pronunciations that are specific to Croatian.

c as the 'ts' in 'cats'
ć as the 'tu' in 'future'
č as the 'ch' in 'chop'
đ as the 'j' in 'jury'
dž as the 'dj' in 'adjust'
j as the 'y' in 'young'
lj as the 'lli' in 'million'
nj as the 'ny' in 'canyon'
š as the 'sh' in 'hush'
ž as the 's' in 'pleasure'

BASICS

Hello.	Zdravo./Bog.
Goodbye.	Doviđenja.
Yes.	Da.
No.	Ne.
Please.	Molim.
Thank you.	Hvala vam/ti. pol/inf
You're welcome.	Nema na čemu.
Excuse me.	Oprostite
Sorry.	Žao mi je.
My name is ...	Zovem se ...
I'm from ...	Ja sam iz ...

ACCOMMODATION

I'm looking for a ...	Tražim ...
guesthouse	privatni smještaj za najam
hotel	hotel
youth hostel	prenočište za mladež

Do you have any rooms available?	Imate li slobodnih soba?
I'd like (a) ...	Želio/Željela bih...(m/f)
bed	krevet
single room	jednokrevetnu sobu
double/twin bedroom	dvokrevetnu sobu
room with a bathroom	sobu sa kupaonicom
How much is it ...?	Koliko stoji ...?
per night	za noć
per person	po osobi

DIRECTIONS

Where is ...?	Gdje je ...?
Go straight ahead.	Idite ravno naprijed.
Turn left.	Skrenite lijevo.
Turn right.	Skrenite desno.

EMERGENCIES

Help!	Upomoć!
There's been an accident!	Desila se nezgoda!
I'm ill.	Ja sam bolestan/bolesna. (m/f)
I'm lost.	Izgubio/Izgubila sam se. (m/f)
Leave me alone.	Ostavite me na miru.
Call a doctor!	Zovite liječnika!
Call the police!	Nazovite policiju!

EATING

I'm a vegetarian.	Ja sam vegetarijanac/vegetarijanka. (m/f)
Waiter!	Konobar!
The menu, please.	Molim vas jelovnik.
What would you recommend?	Što biste nam preporučili?
Please bring the bill.	Molim vas donesite račun.
breakfast	doručak

lunch	ručak
dinner	večera

LANGUAGE DIFFICULTIES

Do you speak (English)?	Govorite/Govoriš li (engleski)? pol/inf
I (don't) understand.	Ja (ne) razumijem.
Can you show me (on the map)?	Možete li mi to pokazati (na karti)?

NUMBERS

1	jedan
2	dva
3	tri
4	četiri
5	pet
6	šest
7	sedam
8	osam
9	devet
10	deset
100	sto
1000	tisuću

SHOPPING & SERVICES

I'm just looking.	Ja samo razgledam.
I'd like to buy (an adaptor plug).	Želim kupiti (utikač za konverter).
May I look at it?	Mogu li to pogledati?
How much is it?	Koliko stoji?
I like it.	Sviđa mi se.
I'll take it.	Uzeću ovo.
Where do I pay?	Gdje se plaća?
Do you accept ...?	Da li prihvaćate ...?
credit cards	kreditne kartice
travellers cheques	putničke čekove
Where's ...	Gdje je ...?
a bank	banka
a public toilet	javni zahod
the tourist office	turistički biro

TIME & DATES

What time is it?	Koliko je sati?
in the morning	ujutro
in the afternoon	poslijepodne
in the evening	navečer
today	danas
tomorrow	sutra
yesterday	jučer
Monday	ponedjeljak
Tuesday	utorak
Wednesday	srijeda
Thursday	četvrtak
Friday	petak
Saturday	subota
Sunday	nedjelja
January	siječanj
February	veljača
March	ožujak
April	travanj
May	svibanj
June	lipanj
July	srpanj
August	kolovoz
September	rujanj
October	listopad
November	studeni
December	prosinac

TRANSPORT

What time does the ... leave/ arrive?	U koliko sati kreće/ stiže ...?
boat	brod
bus	autobus
plane	avion
train	vlak
I'd like a ... ticket.	Želio/Željela jednu ... kartu. (m/f)
one-way	jednosmjernu
return	povratnu
I want to go to ...	Želim da idem u ...
Please stop here.	Molim vas stanite ovdje.

Index

See also separate indexes for Eating (p62), Sleeping (p62), Shopping (p62) and Sights with map references (p62).

A

Adria Adventure 26
Africa 35
agricultural history 16
air travel 51
altars 14
apartments 44
Aquarium 21
architecture 6
   baroque 8, 14, 17, 49
   Gothic 48-9
   Gothic-Renaissance 11, 13, 15, 49
archives 15
art
   modern 16, 50
   Renaissance 11, 14, 50
art galleries 11, 16
Atlas Travel Agency 26

B

Babin Kuk Peninsula 6, 40
bakery 33
Banje Beach 20
bars 35-6, 37
beaches 6, 20, 21, 25, 42, 43, 44
boat travel 51
Bokar Tower 10
bookshops 29
Božidarević, Nikola 11, 50
Bukovac, Vlaho 25, 50
bus travel 51

C

Cafe Buza 35
Café Cele 37
Café Festival 37
cafés 6, 36, 37-8, 54
Capitano 38
Carnival 36
Carpe Diem 35
cars 52
Cathedral of the Assumption of the Virgin 14
cathedrals 14
Cavtat 25
Cervantes 30-1, 35
children
   babysitting 21
   discounts 53
   sights & activities 21, 25, 42
churches 11, 16-17

cinema 36, 38
City Walls 6, 7, 10
classical music 29, 35, 36, 39
climate 52
Clock Tower 9
cloisters 11, 12
clothing 28
clubs 38
consulate 52
Convent of St Clare 18
convents 18
Copacabana Beach 20
craft shops 27-8
credit cards 55
Cro Challenge 36
cuisine 30
culture 36, 38-9, 48
currencies 51, 55
customs regulations 51

D

dance 39
dance music 38
dental services 54
disabled travellers 52-3
discos 38
discount cards 53
districts 6, 40
Dominican Monastery & Museum 11
drink 35-6
   drink shops 29
driving 52
Držić, Marin 38, 49
Dubrovnik Riviera 55
Dubrovnik String Quartet 39
Dubrovnik Symphony Orchestra 39
Dulčić, Ivo 50
duty free regulations 51
DVD 55

E

earthquakes 15, 46
EastWest Club 36
economy 48
EHIC (European Health Insurance Card) 53
Elafiti Islands 26
electricity 53
emergencies 53
entertainment 19, 29, 35-9, 49
environmental issues 47
European Health Insurance Card (EHIC) 53

euros 55
exchange rates 55
Exodus 38

F

Feast of St Blaise 36
ferry travel 51
festivals 19, 36, 39
fish restaurants 30, 31, 32-3, 34
fitness 53
Folklore Ensemble Linđo 39
food & drink shops 29
Frana Supila 6
Franciscan Monastery & Museum 12

G

gay travellers 53
government 47
Gradac Park 21
Gradska Kavana 37
Gruž district 6
Gruž harbour 6
Gundulić, Ivan 20-1, 49
Gundulićeva Poljana 20-1
gyms 53

H

Hamlet 19
health 12, 28, 42, 53-4
Hemingway Cocktail Bar 36
history 10, 15, 17-18, 19, 45-7
holidays 54

I

ID cards 51
insurance 54
International Film Festival 36
International Student Identity Card (ISIC) 53
International Youth Travel Card (IYTC) 53
internet access 54
ISIC (International Student Identity Card) 53
itinerary 7
IYTC (International Youth Travel Card) 53

J

jazz 38, 39
jewellery shop 28
Jewry 17-18
Julian Rachlin & Friends Chamber
    Music Festival 36

K

Karantena Festival 36
Kavana Dubravka 38
kayaking 26
King Richard's Pub 36
klapa songs 29
kunas 51, 55

L

La Boheme 36, 37
Labirint disco 38
language 58-9
Lapad Beaches 20
Lapad Peninsula 6, 40
Latino Club Fuego 38
Lazareti 18-19
left luggage 51
lesbian travellers 53
limestone restoration 48
listings booklet 55
literature 49
Little Onofrio's Fountain 9
Lokrum Island 24
Lopud 25
lost property 54
Lovrijenac Fort 19
luggage 51
Luža Square 9

M

magazines 55
Maritime Museum 16
markets 27
medical services 12, 28,
    53-4
metric conversions 55
Minčeta Tower 10
Mirage 37
Mljet National Park 24
mobile phones 56
monasteries 11, 12, 24
money 51, 55
motorcycles 52
Museum of Modern Art 16
museums 12, 13, 16, 17
music 29, 35, 36, 37, 38,
    39
    music shops 29

N

Navis Underwater Explorers 26
neighbourhoods 6, 40
New Year's Eve Celebration 36
newspapers 55
nightlife 35, 36, 38

O

Old Town 6, 7, 22
Onofrio Fountain 8-9
open-air cinema 38
opening hours 52
Orka 37
Orlando Column 9
orphanage 23

P

parks 21, 24
passports 51
pharmacies 12, 28, 54
phone services 56
phonecards 56
photography 55
    photojournalism 16
Pietà 12
Pile Gate 19
Placa 8-9, 22
Ploče district 40
Ploče Gate 19-20
Poco Loco 37
poetry 20-1, 49
politics 47
pop music 29
post 56
Pracat, Miho 13
private accommodation
    42, 48
Pub Karaka 37
pubs 36, 37

Q

quarantine history 18-19

R

radio 56
Rector's Palace 13
restaurants 30-4, *see also* Eating
    index below
restoration work 48
Revelin Club 38
Revelin Fort 20
Roland (Paladin) 9
roof tiles restoration 48

Roxy 37
Rupe Ethnographic Museum 16

S

St Blaise 17, 19
St Blaise's Church 17
St Ignatius Church 17
St John Fort 18
St Nicholas Church 16-17
St Saviour Church 16
scuba diving 26
security features 10, 18-20, 45
senior citizens' discounts 53
Serbian Orthodox Church &
    Museum 17
Sesame 37
shoes 28
shopping 12, 27-9, *see also*
    Shopping index below
shopping centre 27
sleeping 6, 21, 40-4, 48, *see also*
    Sleeping index below
Sloboda Cinema 38
society 48
Sponza Palace 15
sport 26, 36
star ratings 40
stonemasons' fraternity 23
student discounts 53
Šuica, Dubravka 47
Summer Festival 19, 36, 39
Šunj Beach 25
supermarket 27
Sveti Jakov Beach 21
swimming 42-3
Synagogue 17, 18

T

Talir 38
tapas 30, 35
taxis 51-2
telephone services 56
television 56-7
The Gaffe Pub 36
theatre 19, 38, 39,
    49
time zone 57
tipping 57
toilets 57
tourism 7
tourist information 57
tours 22-6
trading history 15, 45-6
travel documents 51
travel insurance 54
treasury 14
trips 22-6
Troubadur 38, 39
TV 56-7

V

video 55
visas 51

W

War Photos Limited 16
websites 54
wellbeing 42
wine 29
wireless access 54
women travellers 57

Y

youth discounts 53

EATING

Antunini 30
Buffet Skola 30
Cafe Royal 30
Chihuahua Cantina Mexicana 31
Domino 31
Dundo Maroje 31
Eden 34
Kamenice 31
Komin 34
Konavoski Dvori 34
Konobo Atlantic 34
Labirint 31
Levenat 34
Lokando Peskarija 31
Marco Polo 31
Mea Culpa 32
Nautika 32
Orhan 32
Orsan 34
Orsan Yacht Club 34
Pergola 34
Poklisar 32
Porat 32
Posat 32
Proto 33

Ragusa 2 33
Restauracija Konavoka 34
Restaurant Jadran 33
Rozarij 33
Shanghai 33
Spaghetteria Toni 33
Tanti Gusti 33
Tavern Rustica 33

SLEEPING

Apartments van Bloemen 44
Dubrovnik Palace 40
Dubrovnik President 42
Grand Villa Argentina 40
Hilton Imperial 41
Hotel Adriatic 44
Hotel Argosy 42
Hotel Excelsior 41
Hotel Komodor 42-3
Hotel Kompas 43
Hotel Lapad 43
Hotel Minčeta 43
Hotel Perla 43
Hotel Petka 43
Hotel Splendid 43
Hotel Stari Grad 43-4
Hotel Sumratin 44
Hotel Uvala 42
Hotel Zagreb 44
The Pucić Palace 41, 42
Vila Micika 44
Villa Dubrovnik 42
Villa Wolff 42

SHOPPING

Algebra 29
Algoritam 29
Aquarius CD Shop 29
Bačan 27
Deša 27
Franja Coffee & Teahouse 29
Gruž Market 27
Jewellery Gallery Đardin 28
Kadena 28
Konzum 27

Kraš 29
Lapad Shopping Centre 27
Morning Market 27
Pharmacy of the Franciscan
   Monastery 12, 28
Ronchi Hats 28
Vinoteka Dubrovnik 29

SIGHTS

Aquarium 21 (3, F4)
Bokar Tower 10 (3, A3)
Cathedral of the Assumption of
   the Virgin 14 (3, D4)
City Walls 6, 7, 10 (3, B2)
Clock Tower 9 (3, D3)
Convent of St Clare 18 (3, B3)
Dominican Monastery & Museum
   11 (3, E2-3)
Franciscan Monastery & Museum
   12 (3, B2)
Gundulićeva Poljana 20-1 (3, D4)
Lazareti 18-19 (2, F5)
Little Onofrio's Fountain 9 (3, D3)
Lovrijenac Fort 19 (2, E5)
Luža Square 9 (3, D3)
Maritime Museum 16 (3, F4)
Minčeta Tower 10 (3, C1)
Museum of Modern Art 16 (2, F5)
Onofrio Fountain 8-9
Orlando Column 9 (3, B3)
Pile Gate 19 (3, B2)
Placa 8-9, 22 (3, B2-D3)
Ploče Gate 19-20 (3, E2)
Rector's Palace 13 (3, D4)
Revelin Fort 20 (3, F2)
Rupe Ethnographic Museum 16
   (3, B4)
St Blaise's Church 17 (3, D3)
St Ignatius Church 17 (3, C5)
St John Fort 18 (3, F4)
St Nicholas Church 16-17 (3, D3)
St Saviour Church 16 (3, B2)
Serbian Orthodox Church &
   Museum 17 (3, C3)
Sponza Palace 15 (3, D3)
Synagogue 17, 18 (3, D2)
War Photos Limited 16 (3, C3)